THE
ORWELL
ESSAYS

THE ORWELL ESSAYS

A Selection of
Prize-Winning
Journalism

BRIAN SEWELL

QUARTET

First published in 2013 by Quartet Books Limited
A member of the Namara Group
27 Goodge Street, London W1T 2LD
This paperback edition published 2016

ISBN 978 0 7043 7431 7

Typeset by Josh Bryson
Printed and bound in Great Britain by
T J International Ltd, Padstow, Cornwall

CONTENTS

INTRODUCTION

I am now known only as the art critic of the *London Evening Standard*, but from the summer of 1996 until the spring of 2003, I was also one of its columnists, a position given me by the paper's enlightened and generous editor, Max Hastings. His brief to me was no more defined than that I was to express opinion on any serious matter that interested me and that I was not to feel constrained by what the paper's politics might seem to be, nor by the editor's sensibilities. Never had I been so happy and, a muzzled, political animal all my life, I let fly with my opinions, always defended by the editor until he moved on to higher things and was succeeded by Veronica Wadley. She sought abject obedience from me in both subject and opinion, but did not get it, and when, in April 2003 I was awarded the Orwell Prize for my weekly essays, she responded to my disobedience by dropping them.

Had I had to choose between my work as a columnist and my work as a critic, I would have dropped the latter, for I had been so long a critic that I had little new to say, and as a columnist I thought myself capable of a far greater good, uttering a plain man's level-headed response to the follies of Europe and the government, the church, the monarchy and other institutions, expressing a commonsense view on such matters as education, pornography and addiction, and intensely personal opinions

1

THE ORWELL ESSAYS

on our cruel exploitation of animals. To represent them, I have chosen from more than three hundred essays, one in ten.

Brian Sewell, London, 2013

HOMELESS AND HUNGRY
1 OCTOBER 1996

I went yesterday to a modest exhibition of photographs in an all but unknown gallery, not because I recognise photographs as art (I do not), but for their subjects, the homeless young who live on the streets of London. The photographer, Michael Heffernan, moved by their plight, determined to do what he could to draw attention to it and, carrying his camera, a roll of white paper to form a uniform plain background, and a pocket full of £10 notes, recorded not only how the young people look, but how they feel. These images and words are now published in a book sold for the benefit of Shelter, the charitable organisation that gives advice to the homeless, but which can do virtually nothing for the destitute if all hostel beds are occupied.

By chance, and in the comfort of my own home, I have recently attempted to live as a beggar. The exercise began as a test of the value of old age pensions, with the notion that it ought to be possible for an old man to eat and drink sufficiently and wholesomely for £10 a week. It is, but to do so requires a refrigerator, a freezer, a stove and shrewd buying of large loaves, milk by the half-gallon, tea and coffee in the largest packs and searching the supermarket for bacon, cheese, chicken and fish that have had their prices cut as they reach the end of their shelf lives, and may be taken home and frozen. The diet is dull,

3

the chicken invariably boiled to provide soup as well as meat (and not a free-range hen), cabbage the only affordable green vegetable (though with the advantage of infinite variety in the cooking) and root vegetables always chosen by price – carrots are often cheaper than potatoes; tinned chopped tomatoes make a cheap soup and baked beans, bought as a special offer, are a splendid standby.

On the streets of central London, however, this £10 budget for a week cannot be achieved – it is below starvation level. Without the benefit of a kitchen, the beggar is compelled to eat hand to mouth and always buy small quantities because he can keep nothing – once a tin of sardines is open, he must eat them all, and what can he do with a whole raw cabbage? If food and drink are to be warm, then he must pay the going rate – at McDonald's a small coffee and the very smallest hamburger will set him back £1.24, and at Pret a Manger coffee and the cheapest sandwich (egg) cost £1.68. Sandwiches at my local shop are reduced to half price at 4pm, and are a bargain. However, to keep them overnight is to risk a tummy upset.

What does a homeless man do if his bowels betray him? Think on that. How does he keep clean? Where does he shave? Many public lavatories have notices forbidding anything more than washing hands – yet here at home, denying myself the opportunity to bathe, wash, shave or change my clothes, four days see me ripe beyond my own tolerance. How does the homeless man launder his clothes and has he others into which to change? Given the choice of visiting a laundrette or eating, which does he choose? Given that everything he needs, day and night, he must carry and keep with him, does he sacrifice a change of clothing for an extra blanket? – and how often can he launder that? How does he dry his wretched possessions when the rain has caught him unawares?

HOMELESS AND HUNGRY

The margin of discrepancy between the number of hostel beds and the demand for them is unknown; the last survey was carried out in 1991, 8,000 the figure then proposed, the number of homeless counted presumed to be markedly smaller than the true figure. The number of emergency beds has since been cut by the Government, though the quantity of 'move-on accommodation' has been increased – but this is of no use to the absolutely destitute, who must get into a hostel before they are eligible to move on. As the influx of homeless young people into London is constant, it may be supposed that the number committed to living on the streets is now considerably greater than in 1991 – but no one knows.

Those in the direst straits are the very young. At 18, the homeless who have 'moved on' are entitled to Income Support and Housing Benefit (though this last is to be cut from 7 October), but those under 18 have access to no benefit of any kind, and are most vulnerable to prostitution and the doubtful numbing comforts of alcohol and drugs. The Government's response that these young people should not have left home and should return to it, is unrealistic; of the 26 interviews published with Michael Heffernan's photographs, five tell of family rows beyond reconciliation at the ages of 11, 12, 14, 15 and 16, one of a boy nearly killed by his father at the age of 12, one of a boy consistently abused by both parents until taken into care (sometimes an even worse fate), one thrown out by his step-father at 15 and one fleeing from youth custody at 12. These were not spoiled brats rebelling against comfortable middle-class backgrounds, but damaged working-class children of no useful education, fleeing intolerable stress.

Heffernan's attempt to draw attention to their plight has been supported by, among others, Terence Conran, Selfridge's, LWT, The Richard Rogers Partnership, the Economist and

5

Waterstone's – admirable, no doubt, but what is really needed is an immediate increase in hostel accommodation. I argued some years ago in this paper that the Duchy of Cornwall, an extensive landowner in London, could easily set an example and shame the Government; let me now argue that some portion of the Lottery funds should at once be set aside to provide a proper increase in accessible emergency accommodation for the destitute and the dogs that keep them warm and give them company. It should not be beyond the wit of Terence Conran to submit designs and costings. The rest of us could support the projects as best we can, even if only with our signatures and voices.

Every time I visit the Hayward Gallery I encounter the homeless, young and old (the very old often even more pitiable), and am ashamed of a society that can pour so much money into the arts and the architecture frivolities of Millennium celebration, but ignore the indigent. Let the arts and architects go hungry for a while, and now that so much money is slushing about in the Lottery and Millennium funds, let us do something decent and worthy and right for those who have nothing.

CHILD LABOUR
8 OCTOBER 1996

At 10,000ft or so, the steep and narrow hairpin bends blurred by cloud, the autumn cold already bitter in that northernmost tip of Pakistan, reaching to the Hindu Kush, I saw the boy too late to halt the Jeep. Had we run him down it would have been a different matter, but we hadn't, and I doubt if my companions had even noticed him, a slight grey darkness against a paler grey. By the time it was, by English driving standards, possible to pull off the road and deal with the matter, we were far below the boy and I had neither the energy nor the will to return to him.

And what was the matter that in so unlikely a place caused me such anguish that, two years on, I remember it still with stark clarity? It was that the boy, perhaps just into his teens, was begging with an outstretched withered hand, tiny as a baby's, and that his arm too was withered. I dare say that nowadays there is a more politically correct term than withered, but I prefer the word that I learned as a child, Shakespearian and Biblical. It was his right arm too, and the thoughts engendered by it are as fresh as in the moment that I caught his eye and did not pause: first the futility of begging in such a precipitous place on a going-nowhere, dead end, local road, where those from whom he begs are likely to have little more than he, and then the business of growing into adulthood unable to earn the hard-won living of an isolated mountain community where cutting timber and tending goats are the only career prospects for a man; and as for sex – how does such a boy deal with that powerful demand, and the sexual strain that runs so strong in Pathan culture? At that moment, had I been able to stop the Jeep, I would have given him all the money that I had – and that I did not is a regret that will stay with me until my dying day.

I raise this recollection now because, yet again, child labour in the Third World is the subject of hypocritical preaching. Last year we were implored not to buy stone setts to pave our drives and gardens when it was discovered that these are, by tradition, cut and trimmed by families with every small male child joining in at penurious rates of pay. Early this year we were urged to boycott carpets woven in India because small children crawl among the crowded looms, bruising their tiny fingers on the delicate work. Now, it seems, all the famous training boots that, tongues out and laces loose, are the high fashion statement of the very young from Bushey Heath to Bexley, are made hither and yon between Bangkok and the Bosphorus by children just as young, slaving on slave wages. My Pakistani beggar-boy, however, has not the hands to polish a granite sett, nor weave a carpet, nor stitch an expensive canvas boot, and is condemned to begging, crushing penury and hunger, useless to his family.

Moral outrage over child labour in the Third World is itself an outrage. Bring our well-intentioned but utterly ill-considered and self-indulgent European notions to bear in poor countries where child labour is accepted as a part of life, and what do we achieve? Starvation for the very children whom we insist are too young to be employed. Do we really believe that if we take them out of the factories they will be sent to school and taught the tales of Beatrix Potter? Do we really believe that the alternative to child labour is child education and a life of ease among the aspiring middle classes? What arrant nonsense our silly liberalism is.

Beyond the Balkans, in them even, children are not the spoiled and mollycoddled western brats whose lives are ruined if they do not wear the very latest fashion offerings of those who design footwear for Olympic athletes. We do not even have to cross the Bosphorus before, we realise that the economy of mainland Asia, thence to the distant China Seas, is founded on the small boys who attend the working man and learn his trade, and that every factory, dockyard, garage, barber's shop, restaurant, bus station and bazaar would grind to a standstill if forbidden to small boys for whom work is the only serious education they will ever have. We might learn from it, and put our own uncontrollable and ineducable children into such apprenticeships.

The pious souls of western Europe whose consciences still bleed for the horrors inflicted on children during our own Industrial Revolution must be reminded that our society, with all the blessings of the Age of Enlightenment when it began, took two whole centuries and more to convert the horrors of the 18th century into the more or less civilised conditions that obtain today. Our industrial base developed at the pace it did only because wretchedly ill-educated rural peasants were prepared to become an urban peasantry and put their children into mills and factories, or down the mines to work the narrowest seams of ore and coal. Population growth and the availability of grinding; work in conditions no better – indeed, perhaps worse – than cutting cane on West Indian plantations leapfrogged each other, overcrowding, disease, hunger and prostitution shadowing them. These are the conditions now found in the East as nations hasten to become industrial societies, and powerful multi-national manufacturers establish themselves where labour can be had for very little money and no social responsibilities – no sick or holiday pay, no leave for pregnancy, no pensions and no pollution control – and the General Agreement on Tariffs and Trade will make the situation worse. That Rover's new Mini is to be manufactured in Brazil demonstrates the point.

The children of Turkey, Pakistan and India will not thank us for a boycott of their boots, carpets and anything else in which they have a hand, for however badly paid, that is the work that feeds them and teaches them the skills by which they may live when they are adults. Our silly sentimental view of childhood innocence is of no use to them. When negotiating the terms of the Gatt we had the opportunity to better their conditions, but we failed them. In a sense, we failed ourselves too, for the Gatt allows anything to be made anywhere, without protection or proper payment for the labour force, and then without charge or hindrance exported and imported everywhere; multi-national firms must thus be forgiven if they tend to establish themselves where labour is cheap and profit therefore high, even if it means that industrial Europe slips into irreversible decline.

The unromantic traveller in Asia can see for himself the parallels with Britain of 200 years ago. He must accept them, and if he is troubled by the plight of working children, he must buy the boots and carpets that they make, not deplore their making them and demand the closure of the factories. Slaving in their workshops, children are far better off than the Pathan beggar-boy who has so scarred my conscience.

ZIONISM
22 OCTOBER 1996

A hundred years ago, in the spring of 1896, Theodor Herzl, a Viennese journalist, published *The Jewish State*, the pamphlet that established Zionism as a political force.

In advocating an autonomous Jewish settlement in Palestine, he offered a practical response to the anti-Semitism that was rampant in the Austro-Hungarian empire, Germany, Poland, Russia and Romania, often with violent and bloody persecution, and united all the widespread spiritual and theocratic impulses that drove the Jews to dream of a new Judaea to replace the old, destroyed by Roman over-throw in 70 AD.

Zionism may have been a new word in 1896, but it was not a new concept. From Roman times until the late 17th century, pseudo-Messiahs had arisen to preach the restoration of the Jewish State with a prince of the House of David on the throne, and countless medieval persecutions lent strength to this nationalist aspiration.

During Oliver Cromwell's interregnum, the Puritans having shown so much sympathy for the Jews, it was proposed that they should all settle in England as a preliminary to their national re-settlement in Palestine (Cromwell hastily offered them Surinam instead). And some rabbis even supposed that the Protector might himself be descended from King David, perhaps with the idea of enthroning him in Jerusalem, warts, foreskin and all.

In central Europe the issue rumbled on throughout the 18th century, outbreaks of Messianic frenzy alternating with the Judaeophilism of The Enlightenment. It erupted again when Napoleon offered support for a Jewish State in Palestine, and the whole of the 19th century was littered with proposals for settlement there, in England from Lords Shaftesbury and Salisbury, Disraeli and Austen Chamberlain, the Montefiores and the Rothschilds helping to maintain the Jewish agricultural villages eventually established in 1882.

Some Jews argued for 'Spiritual Zionism' rather than a physical home for the Jewish people, but it was the narrow nationalist business of a Jewish State that won the day, given erratic impetus in 1903 by Chamberlain's offer of Uganda instead of the Holy Land (there's an amusing subject for the history game 'What if…?'), and by the Declaration of 2 November 1917, signed by A.J. Balfour, Lloyd George's Foreign Secretary, with which the Jews secured the solemn promise of their Zion.

The promise was not unencumbered; it favoured 'the establishment in Palestine of a national home for the Jewish people', and promised the best endeavours of the British Government in achieving it, but warned 'that nothing shall be done which may prejudice the civil and religious rights of existing non-Jewish communities in Palestine'.

In 1947, after exactly 30 years of riots by the resident Arabs and the arriving Jews, royal commissions, immigration controls and Jewish terrorism of a kind we know well in Northern Ireland, the United Nations declared that there should be separate Jewish and Arab states, with Jerusalem an international enclave – and thus it was that a guilt-ridden world brought into being the State of Israel.

There can be little doubt that Israel has betrayed both the

letter and the spirit of the Balfour Declaration. In 1947 the boundaries of Palestine had defined the country as much smaller than in 1917 and 1896, when, though despairingly described as 'a geographical name of rather loose application', it was mapped as a place of 13 provinces, representing the Twelve Tribes of Israel and the Philistines, with the lands of Asher, Naphtali and Dan reaching far into what are now Lebanon and Syria, and Gad, Reuben and Manasseh occupying a quarter of what is now Jordan.

It was then like Syria, Iraq and Arabia, a province of the Ottoman Empire, and had, in truth, no such clear identity – but whatever its presumed boundaries a century ago, they were not the same as those under the Roman Empire or in far antiquity. For this is a land that has throughout the history of the Eastern Mediterranean, as the crucible of western civilisation, been overrun by powerful neighbours, Hittite, Persian, Egyptian, Assyrian, Greek, Roman and Arab, as well as subject to innumerable internal upheavals and invasions from the West, its borders and its population shifting constantly.

Once Israel was established in this much smaller land, the intellectual folly of Zionism was immediately apparent, for Palestine was not (unlike the Ugandan highlands) empty of people, it was far too small a territory to satisfy the probable demand, and that Jewish occupation could be virtually exclusive was as absurd and menacing a notion as the Aryan purity of Germans.

Zion, that hill of Jerusalem on which the Temple stood, had been a telling metaphor for the spiritual yearning of the Jewish faith, with which all Christian men of poetic mind must have much sympathy, but aggressive territorial occupation of almost every inch once occupied by the Twelve Tribes is a very different matter.

In the 17th century we took to our hearts the pathetic myth of the Wandering Jew as a metaphor of the Jewish Diaspora, and we talk of it now as though we bear the guilt for the Egyptian and Babylonian enslavements as well as the Nazi holocaust.

But Jews wandered and dispersed even when not compelled to do so. St Paul, that most devout of Jews, born in Tarsus, below the Cilician hills of Turkey, preached his new-found Christianity to other Jews long resident in Asia Minor (only Jews could have understood his rants on circumcision). No one compelled the Jews to go to Spain, where they played so significant a part in Moorish culture a thousand years ago. No one drove them to the frozen Baltic, to Venice and to Amsterdam.

That Jews have been seduced by the romantic idea of Zionism is perfectly understandable, but that reasonable men ever sought to translate yearning into physical fact, is not. Israel exists, however, and cannot be undone. Liberal Israelis, fortunate enough to have achieved the dream of Zion, but generous enough to recognise that somehow they must share the land and live in peace with other races and religions, we must support. Illiberal Israelis, heirs to the Zionist aggression of the Thirties and Forties, selfishly and blindly bent on Zionist aggrandisement, and now in the ascendant in Israeli politics, we must deplore, even condemn.

That Europe is guilty of anti-Semitism and the Holocaust, there is no doubt (our tender consciences compelling unjust judgment now and then), but this is no justification for immigrant Jewish abuse of non-Jewish communities in Palestine. Israel should hold to the spirit of the Balfour Declaration.

BATTERY HENS
26 NOVEMBER 1996

Swept aside by noisier news from Westminster last week was a quiet debate in the House of Lords devoted to the welfare of the broiler chicken. The chicken, alas, is not a bird with which we have much sympathy – even Beatrix Potter, who taught most of us to like the hedgehog and the cheeky squirrel, portrays the speckled hen as scatterbrained.

We eat it without a thought, as carelessly as drinking tea or chewing gum, in curries, casseroles and canapés, buns and sandwiches, in pastry cases, polystyrene boxes and unhygienic wicker baskets; we eat it in the street, in Chinese takeaways, in the fast-food emporium and in every caff and cafe in the land. It is a classless food to be found cooked and raw in every supermarket, corn-fed, ready-stuffed, garlic-flavoured, tandoori pink, southern fried, coated with herbs and honey, divided into convenient wings and thighs, breasts and drumsticks. The commonplace of daily diet from Skegness to Bognor Regis, Mumbles to Macduff, we eat some 700 million of these silly, senseless birds each year.

How do we rear these 700 million birds, sentient creatures, every one of them? Are they happily scratching in the hedgerow or strutting in the farmyard? Do they know the seasons and the sun and rain? Do they bathe their feathers in the dust? Do they meet death suddenly, necks wrung by the friendly fanner's wife who scatters corn for them?

The answer to all these questions is a simple 'No', and even to ask them is to suggest that urban man holds to a notion of decent animal husbandry that has become a distant folk memory, the stuff of fairy-tales, for agriculture is now a murky business in which subsidy and profit are not only the driving forces, but the only things that matter to the farmer, of whom, for reasons beyond reasoning, all politicians are afraid.

Over the past 40 years, the techniques of industrial mass-production have invaded the farm, bringing systematic cruelty on cows and calves, sheep and lambs, pigs and piglets, in the interest of greatly increased output, at the same time reducing the labour force to a tenth of what it was. Those who have valiantly opposed the routine barbarity of what is now called agribusiness, have, by the steady drip drip of compassion on the stone, begun to affect for the better the welfare of the larger animals, but the poor hen is still neglected, the only creature not yet protected by one single law.

Chris Mullin MP, in a General Bill pleading for decency, brought their plight to the notice of the Commons in July, but we have heard no more of it. Last week, however, Lord Beaumont of Whitley presented in the Lords the Welfare of Broiler Chickens Bill, and we shall hear a little more of that, for with the second reading unopposed, it goes to the committee stage and, unless defeated by lordly spokesmen for the industry, may well, with a little luck, be debated in the Commons. Chickens for the oven and the pot are reared in huge barrack sheds without windows, as many as 30,000 in each, the noise, stench and heat unbearable to any human being. Overfed and deprived of all natural activity, they grow and fatten fast, but their bones are soft, bending under the weight they carry, and when the birds are slaughtered on the 42nd day of their wretched lives, they have experienced great pain in joints and muscles, and, incapable of walking, may only have moved by dint of flapping their wings and pushing themselves about on their breasts – this in the deep, damp litter of wood shavings and shit accumulated over six weeks and never cleaned or changed. Even worse treatment is meted to hens reared for their eggs, for they spend their entire lives confined in battery cages so small that they can neither walk nor spread their wings.

The unhappy broiler chicken is not a healthy bird. Some seven million die of congestive heart failure and abdomens filled with body fluids, but with 30,000 in his flock, the husbandman may never see their corpses. Countless birds develop blistered breasts and ulcerated legs caused and made worse by pushing about and squatting in their filthy litter; sampling indicates that half the national flock of 700 million birds are infected with salmonella or campylobacter, the prime sources of food poisoning in humans, and that one third, if properly inspected in supermarkets, should be condemned as unfit for human consumption.

Removal to the slaughterhouse brings appalling trauma to the birds. The industry's deceitful euphemism for the process is 'harvesting', conjuring an old-fashioned image of the sunlit farm, the farmer in his smock, his plump wife in her pinny; the brutal reality is that a team of catchers invades the barn, each of whom gathers at least four birds in each hand, caught by one leg only, to cram them into crates for what is often a very long and terrifying journey to the slaughterhouse. This rough handling breaks legs and dislocates hips, with acute pain and haemorrhage; in crating the injured birds, broken bones often enter their abdominal cavities; many die of these injuries, and many more of heart failure. In the slaughterhouse the rough handling continues, the birds shackled upside-down to a production line on which, with luck, they are stunned before their throats are cut and they are scalded for de-feathering; 30 per cent are luckless.

The duck and the turkey suffer the same callous barbarities as the chicken. The natural life-span of the duck is 20 years, the turkey's 10, a chicken's six – but agribusiness gives the duck eight weeks without even a pool in which to paddle, the turkey six months, the chicken 42 days: can this and the attendant unrelenting cruelties be morally justified in the interests of cheap food and monstrous profit? The Government's answer is a resounding 'Yes', its response to Lord Beaumont's Bill that it is too expensive – that to limit the size and density of flocks would cost the industry £150 million more a year, with veterinary fees an extra £400 million, and other matters bringing the total to £1 billion, and that this makes reform impossible. What kind of society is this, when we do not even pretend to have values? Why is the Conservative Party so scared of locking horns with these rural Nazis, when far more votes are to be won in urban constituencies by imposing reforms on agribusiness?

Let us then begin only with limiting the size and density of flocks, a bargain at £150 million spread over 700 million birds, a mere 20 pence a chicken. Evidence of that modest reform will lie in the straight bones of thigh and drumstick on our plates. Then, year by year, let us go further with reform until nothing in our animal husbandry brings shame on us – with easy stages, even the heartless farmers will scarcely feel the pain.

URBAN SPRAWL
26 DECEMBER 1996

That the citizens of Somerset are to be encouraged to erect boundaries about their county, with the notice 'You are now entering a pensioner-free zone' at every picketed turnpike, the stout yeomanry ready to repulse all who bear a bus pass, is faintly ludicrous. It has the air of an Ealing Comedy, perhaps, or of a newly-discovered sequel to Swift's tales of Lilliput and Brobdingnag, and has been greeted with derision – but is it entirely absurd that those born and bred in what was once one of Britain's most picturesque and romantic counties Bath and the Mendip Hills to the east, wild Exmoor to the west, should wish it to retain something of the rural character it had when they were young? Why should their ancient market towns be riven with pedestrian precincts, their domestic scale be overwhelmed with gigantic shopping malls, and be skirted with a broad band of ugly bungalows, simply to satisfy the unreal retirement dreams of city-dwellers from the alien north who want roses round the cottage door without having to surrender a jot or tittle of urban convenience?

The Government's prediction that over the next two decades more than four million houses must be built, is one that we should heed with alarm, demanding urgent revision of our housing policies. These are to be, not new houses to replace the crumbling urban stock (that is an unacknowledged problem of even greater menace), but new houses to encroach on the green fields between country towns and villages, new houses to erode the Green Belt that has skirted London almost inviolate for more than half a century, a nationwide development that will swiftly destroy all the rural pleasures and delights that are the very things that urban man believes he most desires when he retires to the country. Urban man is the agent and instrument of Suburbia Triumphant.

Town planning has been stuck in the mud since the beginning of the century, and is still dominated by the dreams of William Morris. The density of population in those areas of these islands where most people now want or need to live and work, demands a new approach. We cannot continue to think in terms of Morris's green and leafy Chiswick and Hampstead Garden Suburb as the best ways of permitting urban sprawl; we must not build more wasteful garden cities like Welwyn, Letchworth, Harlow and the execrable Milton Keynes; we must not, panic-stricken by demand, destroy the close-knit character of cathedral cities, market towns and slow-grown villages with planning permission for urban sprawl and supermarkets utterly alien in architectural vernacular. If we do not change our ways at once, we shall irreversibly destroy the countryside – and in doing so, we shall, almost without noticing, destroy our major cities too.

Look about you in London at the means adopted in the past to deal with demand and density – means now largely neglected, but worth reviving. Look at Baton Square with its tall terraces looking onto leafy communal gardens, where the upper classes (so they think) live at close-quarters and even the basements are desirable *pieds-a-terre*. Look at Albany, a bleak barracks for old lords and ladies (or so it used to be) hiding to the north of Piccadilly – more close quarters. Look at the red brick mansion blocks that huddle in the shadows of Westminster Cathedral, and look at the cobbled mews, the servants' quarters now made good – still more close quarters.

Look at Bath, a World Heritage City, designed in the 18th century to an ideal plan that acknowledged the essential difference between town and country, and at its heart still breathtaking in beauty and function. Look at the work of Le Corbusier, the greatest thinker of this century in terms of town planning, whose solutions and designs were, alas, damnably ugly and oppressive 'machines for living', but who recognised that the purposes of town and country are fundamentally opposed, and that there should be a sharp edge to every city.

To save the countryside from urban invasion (nothing will save it from the farmers) we must first regenerate our cities. Our fundamental error lies in the planners' belief that we are all equal, making the same demand for housing within our social band. We are not, and we do not, and the notion that two down, three up, somewhere for the car, a mock Georgian porch (very mock), a front garden and a back is a demand born in our genes, is simpleminded, if not downright lunatic. Too many people do indeed have this idée-fixe, but only because they have no notion of the alternatives, and know nothing of, for example, the convenience of having 11 rooms on one floor, the ceiling lofty, the balconies large enough for cucumber sandwiches and tea.

The town planners of the Sixties made the tower block disreputable, and in doing so did an appalling damage to urban redevelopment in Britain, for the tower block is our only hope. How is it that we admire and envy the skyscrapers and condominiums of New York, but loathe their equivalents here? It is because they are ugly in their placing and their relationships with each other and buildings that are older and smaller in scale, because they are hideous in design, mean in their proportions, wretched in their materials, and shoddy in detail – true not only of the prefabricated and predestined slums built for the working classes with their inherent condensation problems, broken lifts and mean public areas, but of those intended for the moneyed, as in the Barbican, which is as bleak, tawdry and ill-designed a development as any this side of the Urals.

The Barbican, however, recognises one essential of the decent urban plan – that in distancing our places of work from those of domestic bliss, we are in grave error, generating traffic, compelling ourselves to waste hours of every day in needless travel to our dormitory towns (a telling term indeed), destroying leisure, and adding to exhaustion. Imagine cities in which we could walk to work, with the consequent drop in pollution, noise and congestion; it requires not only the radical revision of our planning constraints, but of the very way in which we think of buildings.

Architects and developers must learn once more how to give dignity to the communal parts of buildings – to inspire awe with entrance halls and staircases (the most exciting and multi-dimensional elements in all architecture); the passage and the corridor must be much more than warrens of access and communication, touched with style and grandeur. Then they must learn to mix many purposes in a single building – Canary Wharf, for example, could accommodate a sixth-form college, a cottage hospital, a sports complex, a public library and public offices, as well as business premises and private housing, and throw in theatres, restaurants and cinemas too. We must learn to build urban villages where residents have all the advantages of urban life along the corridor.

Above all, we must learn to celebrate our urban life. It need not be all traffic jams and filthy air, the crush and rat run of the

URBAN SPRAWL

Underground and main-line terminus. It could be a 10-minute walk to an airy apartment on the umpteenth floor of a block so well constructed that no sound penetrates from neighbours – a walk shaded by great plane trees, past open-air cafes in secluded garden squares. Our town planners have forgotten, if they ever knew, how to plan towns, and invariably inflict on us the suburb – the one concept that does most damage to both city and the country. Let us pronounce anathema on every bungalow and executive estate; the city should end abruptly, fronting a vista of green fields as a cliff drops to the sea, and the green fields should be inviolate. Let us praise the city and adapt it so that none of us will ever dream of retirement in Somerset.

SLEEPING ROUGH
14 JANUARY 1997

How unfortunate our senior politicians are. Assiduously they cultivate their images as Honest John or Clean-limbed Jack, smiling like a Pavlov dog at every passing pensioner and baby, always reassuring everyone that if we do not already live in the best of all possible worlds, then leave it to them and soon we shall, outdoing Martin Luther King with dreams and Wellington with practicalities, laying claim to the spiritual life with regular observance in the House of God as well as Commons, creatures of the Cardinal Virtues as well as Faith, Hope and Charity, and then all is suddenly undone by some wretched scribbler from the Press who catches a great man in a rare unwary moment, revealing a fissure in the carefully constructed edifice of rectitude and decency.

Consider Anthony Blair's predicament when Simon Rogers called to interview him for *The Big Issue*. Rogers put it, he was friendly and chatty, 'yet obviously preoccupied' – and that preoccupation cost him dear. In talking of the homeless, the very issue that is the origin and being of that magazine, he fell into the fundamental error of treating the homeless, the vandal and the mugger as a single problem, and uttered emphatic support for the Zero Tolerance that has been so successful in New York. He then compounded the error by boasting that he never gives to beggars.

SLEEPING ROUGH

A momentary lapse from his normal acuity of mind, a touch of boredom with the interview perhaps, a chance intrusive thought of the Colefax and Fowler curtains he will have in number 10, and out slip the unwary words, unnoticed by himself, but noted by the journalist. Once published, other wretched scribblers, out to get him (persecution mania is all too common to all politicians who think undiluted praise their only deserved and wholesome diet), pounce, and with what he condemns as careful selection and spiteful gloss, he is made to seem a pious prig descended not from Mrs Do-as-you-would-be-done-by but Mrs Be-done-by-as-you-did.

As one of those meretricious scribblers he accuses me of distorting the facts of what he said. He did not, he claims, utter 'a general condemnation of the poor'. I have no doubt that he did not intend to, but in the recorded interview, he says 'I'm saying we do have to make our streets safe for people,' a statement with which none can argue, but he immediately follows it with 'Obviously the way to do that is to tackle the reasons why those people are sleeping on the streets.'

In his response to me he wrote '…what I said, and I stand by 100 per cent, is that the answer to homelessness is not tolerance of crime.' There we have it, twice – the unmistakable bracketing of homelessness with crime, implying that if we get the homeless off the streets, crime will disappear, and conversely, if we put all petty criminals in gaol, we shall never see another homeless beggar. If that is the level of your logic Mr Blair, then you don't deserve to be Secretary of State for Interior Decoration, let alone Prime Minister.

You object to my association of you with the term 'Young Barbarians', and claim that you never said it. I did not say that you had, but young Simon Rogers asked you directly if you agree with Frank Field's observations on 'Young Barbarians, a lawless generation … drawn to crime' (perhaps I should remind you that Frank Field is one of your MPs), and you replied at some length with, 'What Frank is suggesting, and I think the basic premise is right…' If the term Young Barbarians is so objectionable, you could and should have said so, but you accepted it without demur – though I dare say that you were thinking about new lampshades and chandeliers for Number 10.

You object to my assertion that you conjure a 'threatening image of the aggressive beggar', but you did specifically imply that in the interview 'I often drop my kids off at King's Cross … and it's actually quite a frightening place…', not in answer to a question on street crime, but to one restricted to begging. Are we also to see you, Mr Blair, heartless as a father, tipping your children out of the chauffeur-driven Rover at King's Cross, the poor tots in fear and trembling, because you are in a haste to get to Harrods and order pale pink fitted carpets for your rooms in Number 10?

Your interview in *The Big Issue* revealed a grave flaw in your judgment, and a decent politician (if such a creature exists) would at once have acknowledged it. Your response, however, was disingenuous, dissembling, and as frothy as most of what you say on every matter now.

There are two separate problems on the streets – one is crime, the other poverty; there may be an area of overlap, but the destitute whom I have encountered are not criminal in even the smallest degree, and the criminals are not even poor, let alone homeless and destitute. I loathe the Americanism Zero Tolerance, and imagine that it is fashionable among the politically correct of Camden and the Chianti-quaffing chatterers of Islington (otherwise you wouldn't use it), but if it means that you have a policy poised for action as soon as the Poggenpohl kitchen has been installed at Number 10, and the streets really will be cleared of muggers and the boys who steal the radios and wheels from our cars, then more strength to your elbow, Mr Blair, as you raise best bubbly to your lips in the early hours of a day in May. But shop doorways will still be the shelters of the poor, for this is another problem altogether, for which you offer not a single sure and certain remedy.

Throughout your response to what you describe as my vitriol, you return time and again to your fundamental error, speaking of the poor and the criminal as one. It may be that the poor are always to be with us – that is indeed my view, and those of us who live in comfort have a duty to ameliorate their poverty. To talk of 'high quality education and skills', and to pledge that they will have immediate access to 250,000 jobs, is fraudulent – if it were so easy, would unemployment be rising in the best-managed societies in Europe? No, Mr Blair, you can pour as much money as may be into skills and education, but it will not create a single job – it will merely force the educated destitute into competition with all those university graduates who cannot, for all their high degrees, find work to fit their abilities.

But I forgive you, Mr Blair, for though you have no workable solution for the problem of the destitute, and offer only the self-deceit of waffle, at least you don't take David Maclean's Conservative view that the poor are poor because they want to be so, nor do you embrace the solution proposed by his mate and mucker Terry Dicks, who would power-hose them from shop doorways. And anyway, I imagine that you did not pen that piece yourself for the *Evening Standard* last week, but, too intent on selecting pictures from the National Gallery for Number 10 (a deplorable prerequisite for all Prime Ministers nowadays), appointed one of your many minions to the task, perhaps a bright young graduate from the LSE on a work experience scheme, capable of adopting your house style. You'd have been wiser, however, to offer two words of apology yourself, not to me but to all the destitute you accuse of being criminal, and promise to give a fiver to every beggar you pass – but alas, you are always in your chauffeur-driven Rover, practicing to be Prime Minister.

SCHOOL SOCIETIES
28 JANUARY 1997

One of the privileges, responsibilities or mere consequences of rising from the third to the fourth form at my school, and thus from the Lower to the Upper half, was compulsory membership of Combined Cadet Force. It had long been the OTC, the Officers' Training Corps, but some post-War egalitarian nonsense had crept into the school's low church psyche and, in responding to the insistence of a few boys that their patriotism could be more properly expressed at the joystick of a Spitfire, the school's corps had diversified into grey-blue as well as khaki uniforms and been re-christened the CCF. No one in my day showed any interest in the Navy, though that was the most obvious destination for so many little whores.

The CCF paraded one afternoon a week, expected to know its left from right and to respond with alacrity to the yelps and curdled screams emitted by strutting masters in peaked caps and big boys with sergeant's stripes. This formality done, the Air Force boys disappeared into the science block to grasp the mysteries of aeronautics; the rest of us in ill-fitting khaki hand-me-downs first worn by midgets in the 1914-18 war (the smallest boys wore puttees, a bandage from knee to ankle that came undone with too much stamping) ran about the playing-fields with rifles that had seen service at Khartoum, or were dragooned hither and yon in calamitous drill movements. To the sensitive soul it seemed no better than bullying by prefects, licensed by loathsome masters who could not see what prigs the big boys were, nor that everything they did was no better than sucking up to their authority.

We suffered worse and more of it on field days, carried off in three-ton trucks to crawl in mud and dust while malevolent masters tossed thunderflashes at our heels. The remedy for these was to make for a hedge or ditch within distant sight of the trucks and lie low for the day until the company reassembled, then to join it for the homeward journey with: 'Sorry Sir. Got lost Sir. Separated Sir. Don't know Sir. Sorry Sir…' How I loathed the need for such obsequiousness.

Risen to the lower sixth, I took part in a revolt with a dozen Jewish boys. They claimed religious objection to the Corps and, getting away with this excuse, learned bone-setting and first aid instead of the clumsy skills of war; my conscientious objection, however, was (rightly) not believed, and I was punished. My resolve not broken by conventional punishments, I was sent off on 100-mile cycle rides, alone, with the requirement that I draw a well-known church or country house as proof of the journey, or despatched to Bisham Abbey, again by bike, to spend the day turning turtle and righting a canoe.

How mistaken my masters were. I learned more of endurance, tenacity and willpower from being upside-down in the Thames than ever from the discomforts of mud and thunderflashes, and far more of self-trust from those exhausting explorations on my bike. I needed no lessons in loyalty to the wretched school – that had come with playing rugger, the most physical and desperate of games, and with long-distance running. I needed no pseudo-military lessons in the larger loyalty of patriotism when I had these abilities. As for leadership – the Holy Grail of all who have in the past week praised the Prime Minister's notion that all schools should now have cadet forces – that comes more readily from a school's intellectual societies than from playing soldiers in the rain. Teach a boy to debate and you have given him a far more useful tool than any rifle. Teach him to perform in drama and you have given him confidence. Teach him to sing or play an instrument before his peers and you have removed a formidable fear. Teach him the skills of team games and he will know all that he needs of corporate loyalty and responsibility to others.

It is an irony that education authorities have in recent years maintained that there must be neither winners nor losers in their schools, and that competitive games and examinations are damaging to society. It is an irony that in the current debate on education there should be so much prating of literacy and numeracy, but no one mentions the need to be articulate, to marshal arguments and give clear voice to matters passionately felt. Yet it is not unreasonable to claim that in the adult world the extra-mural activities of a school prove to be of far greater use and benefit than any academic subject dully taught, for it is these that draw out and strengthen inherent character.

If the Government can find the money to support newly-instituted cadet forces with uniforms, arms and the assistance of professional soldiery (for no teachers now have had military experience), it can with better purpose and result support school societies, choirs, orchestras and sports, all of which will lead to the life-long enrichment of leisure. The only reasonable purpose of a cadet corps is the ready provision of recruits for the armed forces, laudable enough during the last war and the long years of National Service, but so utterly pointless now that only generals and marshals retired to rose-clad cottages in Scrotum Magna could waffle their acclaim and think John Major a good egg. No doubt his next move to restore Conservative confidence will be the resuscitation of the Primrose League – guaranteed to be a wow with all doubters over 80.

The revival of National Service rather than the CCF one might view with sympathy. National Service took vast numbers of young men out of the unemployment pool for two full years and taught them responsibility for themselves, for their platoon and company, and the complex webs of trust, unhesitating reliance and support on which every military unit must depend. Most learned a skill or trade that was to stand them in good stead in civvy street. Most grew very fast from riotous and rebellious boys into responsible men, and society was safer and less selfish for what the Army did for them. There is no place for it now, and without its inexorable discipline nothing could function in its stead – but in its day it did a great good for society, and few of us made our way home from our last camp without a sense of deep regret, knowing that a vital chapter of our lives had ended. For that grave experience the CCF is a ludicrous substitute.

EDUCATION
24 JUNE 1997

One of the many plagues of present-day London is that of the boys who hawk dusters and other household trifles on our doorsteps. There they stand, pathetic and imploring, with an assortment of inflammable oven gloves and aprons, covers that fit no ironing-board in Christendom, scissors guaranteed to cut cola cans in half but useless for any serious purpose, and an assortment of kitchen commonplaces of wretched quality at twice the price of far better things in Harrods.

Some break into a rehearsed patter that is as unstoppable as was Mrs Bottomley's record when prating of good causes; others, at the end of a long day, exhausted, simply look at the householder in mute misery and the forlorn expectation of the brusque 'Be off with you.'

It was one of these last who rang my doorbell on Saturday as the light was fading – a woebegone waif, everything about him speaking of fatigue and disappointment. He began his spiel, and I began my 'No, no, no …,' which always ends with a charitable 'Hang on a minute and I'll give you something to see you on your way'. At this he brightened a little, and then said: 'I know you. You're that art critic.' I should by now be more or less accustomed to this recognition, but I still blush, and I still do not know why I am that and not merely the or an art critic – that, said with peculiar emphasis, carries unrecognisable connotations. He then said: 'I'm sick of doing this. I suppose you couldn't get me a job on the paper?' Life was so simple when Kenneth Grahame wrote *The Wind in the Willows* 90 years ago, a book at least as much an influence on my moral philosophy as the New Testament; Mr Badger could welcome young hedgehogs into his sett and give them porridge, and Mole could reward the carolling field mice with fresh savoury comforts in his dining-room, but this was not what was required of me – this stray ragamuffin was asking for a job, a gift beyond my giving. My spirit bleak, I said lamely that I would see what I could do – 'Write me a letter telling me everything about yourself, listing your qualifications…' but he cut me short – he has none. At 16 he has passed no examination in any subject, and though he can do simple arithmetic, can barely read and write – 'I can do joined-up writing if I try hard and do it very slowly.'

'Grief,' I thought to myself, 'what use are you to a newspaper?' but forebore to say it. Here we have a boy, neat, presentable, endowed with cockney cunning and not without wit, who has had 11 years of education at the taxpayer's expense and has derived from it no significant benefit. What has it cost to put this boy through the state system? And what is he still to cost the taxpayer in unemployment, housing and other benefits for which he may be eligible over the next half century or so? – this larger secondary cost all but inevitable as a consequence of the failure of professional teachers to teach him. The cost in money can be measured, but important though it is in the general argument on education, appealing to accountants, the immeasurable costs in social suffering should anger us far more, for the failure of an education system is a stupid crime against humanity – a crime committed by past governments of both political complexions, their dogma, prejudice, envy and spite masquerading as educational philosophies, by bigoted local authorities who presume the political correctitudes to be the essences of education, and by self-interested unions of teachers most concerned with protecting their members no matter how incompetent, inadequate and themselves the victims of a wretched education.

In comprehensive schools we have developed an education system better suited to the battery hen than children. It may gain the economies of scale, but it loses the close intimacy of teacher and pupil through which an aptitude may be recognised and made to flourish. It was designed to offer equality of opportunity – a notion as fallacious as the assumption that in giving the same running shoes to me as Linford Christie uses, I should do as well at Crystal Palace – and the unequal child, the floundering and failing child, is lost in such a system.

Education, we were assured by all political parties at the May hustings, is the matter dearest to them; they all agreed that education is in the doldrums, that far too many children leave school illiterate and innumerate, condemned to a level of brute labour that no longer exists in this country, and thus to permanent unemployment; there is general agreement that something must be done about it, and the pious hope that if we throw enough money at the problem it will at once be solved; and there is touching faith in a national curriculum that will equip all adolescents for a world of full employment that is gone forever, with computer skills and other technical trivialities now demanded by employers. They all make the fundamental error of mistaking training for education, and fail to recognise that those who truly educate open the doors to perception, give their pupils the academic tools and disciplines with which to discover for themselves, and then let them make an informed choice. Aptitude and interest are the driving forces that children themselves contribute to their education, creatures of wide-eyed wonder that must be nurtured by teachers if they are not to perish in the slough of boredom and neglect.

Alas we recognise aptitude only when it is at its most extreme – in dance and music; for no other disciplines are there special schools, not even the visual arts, and precocity is restrained, even suppressed. An aptitude for languages is one that we should recognise with joy, for it is the gateway to all other cultures – yet we are the most monoglot of nations, scorning even the ability to speak and write our own, clinging with inverse snobbery to the notion that the ugly accents of Liverpool and Birmingham are better than a received pronunciation that reflects the literary form and is intelligible worldwide. Has it occurred to no educational expert that the ability to read and write must to some considerable extent depend on the ability to speak with accuracy? I have heard teachers and education experts in the past few days refer to eddication, the Seckertary of State and Parliament, and have wondered how their pupils might fare in a dictation test.

I do not suppose for one moment that the Prince of Wales ever opens his front door to be confronted by a boy selling dusters ('I know you, you're that Prince'), but his recent venture into the education debate was pointed and well worth the venturing. It was received with the inevitable huffs and puffs of resentment and wounded complacency by the ill-spoken nincompoops who speak for most of the profession, and then, alas, lost in the welter of reporting on the Amsterdam conference and the Tory leadership. The debate he raised must not be allowed to die away, nor must it be left in the hands of the professionals who for the best part of 40 years have served the young so badly and cost the state so much, and wastefully.

EDUCATION

This self-satisfied profession should be purged of dross. It should be more difficult to become a teacher, the profession no longer the safe haven of the academic failure and the mindlessly unambitious. Its status raised, it should be far better paid. It should not be burdened with bureaucracy, nor any good headmaster turned into a clerk. Above all, not only should classes be much smaller but so should schools; if one factor more than any other has brought about the failure of the comprehensive school, it is the sheer scale of it, the great number of its pupils and its anonymity. New Labour should not merely tinker with the system and juggle out of existence expensive school places that will almost certainly result in long-term unemployment, but tackle the whole business root and branch, with a new philosophy. Meanwhile, what can I do for the boy who stood on my doorstep if, with enormous effort, he sends me a letter in his joined-up writing?

GONERIL, REGAN
AND LADY MACBETH
18 NOVEMBER 1997

Men of a certain age, brought up to doff their hats to women, open doors for them, bow and scrape and put them into lifeboats first, cling to these conventions at the risk of being set aside as old fogeys and old buffers blind to the social revisions of the past 30 years. They are forbidden by political correctitude to think of women as the fair and gentle sex whom they must revere, nor are they allowed to see them as sexually willing wenches whose bottoms they may pinch. No doubt some polytechnic academic has composed a doctoral thesis on the paradox of the creature who in the mythology of men is on the one hand the devoted little woman, dutiful wife and loving mother of their children, and on the other is mopsy, doxy, strumpet and trollop happy to accommodate a man at any moment, even standing up in a canoe.

These concepts persist, for they are rooted deep in an inheritance that reaches far back beyond the mythology of ancient Greece, but against these millennia of entrenched traditional attitudes, we have set one generation of feminist argument and wrought a formidable change that leaves many a man disoriented. Though governed, as all men are to some considerable extent, by his unruly member, he may not utter certain words or sentiments, may not touch or gesture, for the concept of woman as doxy is now done for by law and politics. The other concept of woman, as warm, kindly and compassionate, as the mother of us all, as the comforter for whom grown men cry on deathbed and in deep distress, still stands fairly firm, but for some of us is blemished by their attitude to abortion, cosmetics and fur coats, for in all three, women demonstrate a measure of heartless selfishness quite alien to the image of woman as universal mother. To many men it is incomprehensible that in the 30 years since abortion was made legal, some five million foetuses, living human beings whose hearts are functioning and limbs are formed, far from the mere blobs of jelly of which pro-abortionists so often speak, have been ripped from wombs with the compliance and authority of law and medicine. Are women quite so often sexually had against their will?

That an abortion may save a woman's sanity when she has been assaulted by a stranger, drunk, drugged and perhaps diseased, we may feel compelled to concede, but that abortion should be employed as a primary method of birth control – and that is the implication of this huge and growing number – is surely not acceptable. Convenience was the reason for 91 per cent of abortions in 1996 – unwanted babies dressed up in the statistics as supposed threats to the physical and mental health of mothers. These were babies that need not, and should not, have been conceived, but prevented with a moment's forethought and the necessary simple apparatus to keep egg and sperm apart.

The Roman Catholic Church has, rightly, much to say on the matter, but is wrong-footed by its attitude to birth control. Were it to concede that to frustrate the consequence of lust with a condom or a pill is, if not virtuous, only a sin of trifling weight compared with murdering a child in the womb, and were it to change to a policy of education advocating more effective means of birth control than pious hope, we might well find a significant reduction in abortions. Far the greater burden of responsibility, however, must lie with women themselves, for most care not a fig for the opinions of popes and cardinals, and if they do not want to be twinned with Medea in our minds, then they must be, at the very least, a little less careless with their congress.

It is time that we questioned the fancy that women are more compassionate and merciful than men. Are they indeed in any sense the gentler sex? They have for years ignored the cruel business of cosmetic testing on small animals that in cuddly woollen form they give as comforts to their children, their eyes closed to the tears wept by rabbits blind with pain deliberately inflicted; it is in the face of massive indifference that this is now to end. Worse, the filthy trade in furs survives and increases solely for the vanity of women – a trade in wild animals indiscriminately trapped and, in animals bred for slaughter, fed on each others' bodies, kept in cages so small and conditions so vile that, in comparison, the farmer who breeds broiler chickens might think he runs a Ritz for his miserable hens.

Do women care nothing for such endangered species as the snow leopard? Nothing for a wild animal slowly dying of cold and hunger in a snare or trap? Is their vanity of such overwhelming importance to them that it overrides the compassion they should feel for the captive victims of the loathsome breeding trade in Canada, America, Russia, Scandinavia and even in this country? How do they think these animals are killed? Kindly, by a man trained in humane slaughter? Not at all – slaughter in this country and most others requires no training, no certificate of skill; the more fortunate animals receive a lethal injection, but these are few; some have their necks broken with a karate chop, others gasp their lives away with the stink of vehicle exhaust fumes in their nostrils. The least fortunate animals are electrocuted because that way their coats are best preserved – and how is that done? With one electrode jammed in the anus and the other in their jaws.

Eight years ago the Farm Animal Welfare Council observed that the systems employed in the farming of mink and fox do not satisfy some of the most basic criteria for protecting the welfare of cows and pigs and hens. Nothing has changed since then. The Ministry of Agriculture has shown no interest in the welfare of these essentially wild animals, inquisitive and intelligent predators whose strong natural instincts lead to great suffering when caged, with appalling signs of stress. In America, so considerable is the demand for fur that breeders are experimenting with a wider range of caged animals – beaver, wolverine and lynx now added to the mink and fox, for the estimated worldwide production of 25 million mink and three million fox each year is not enough to satisfy the demand – and the demand is made by women, not by men.

Perhaps we should not expect women to be troubled by the deaths of so many animals when they so readily trot off to the abortionist to rid themselves of children. Why should killing an animal, caged or in the wild, mean anything unpleasant to a woman whose response to an unwanted pregnancy is to have it liquidated? Men, who learn their reverence for women at their mothers' knees have been misled by at least 3,000 years of propaganda and find it very difficult to acknowledge that women are, if not the physically tougher sex, certainly the more coldly selfish, calculating and manipulative, far the more capable of pulling down the shutters of their minds when something unpleasant stands in the way of ambition or desire. They have insidiously achieved abortion on demand and are unlikely to relinquish it, but they could retain something of their ancient reputation for kindness and compassion if they would unite against the fur; overnight their unity could end this trade in bloodstained vanity.

FOX HUNTING
25 NOVEMBER 1997

In not one of my many years – and I now look forward to all the privileges of dotage – have my views been sought by pollsters on the popularity of Prime Ministers and tinned baked beans, though I have strong views on both. I am thus mistrustful when I am told that 61 per cent of us is vehemently opposed to fox-hunting – a figure that will be much bandied about this coming Friday, when Mr Michael Foster's bill to end the pursuit of the stag and fox with hounds is debated in the Commons.

Against stag-hunting my views are indeed vehement – a callous business, shaming our humanity, intellectually indefensible. I am against fox-hunting too, but my views are less absolute. Thirty years ago, when the saboteur was rare, I did my bit to disrupt the local hunt, for it so obviously played no spiritual part in our society, but appealed only to beastly and unwholesome instincts. Like all field sports it provides an adrenal rush, a thrill, but unlike some it provides nothing for the pot or oven, and in touching the same dark parcel of our primeval nature that exults in the lynching of a criminal, it rouses that which should now be in desuetude or dormant; it is as distasteful to the civilised man as any Spanish business with the bull, and is, in its customs, dress codes, language and the sounding of its horns, as arcane a ritual. It must be stopped, but not yet, not now, for worthy principle will not save the life of one single fox, and death by the chase – which to some extent the wily fox must comprehend – will be replaced by gassing, trapping, shooting, digging, cubbing, forms of death beyond his comprehension, and from which, unlike the hunt, there is not the slightest possibility of escape for him, his vixen or his cubs.

The 314 registered packs of hounds, of which 200 hunt the fox, work between October and mid-March, some as many as four times a week, some only once – some 20,000 dogs in all, including 14,000 foxhounds and 200 staghounds, the remainder beagles, mink hounds and the harriers used in mounted hare hunting (the very idea of hunting the harmless hare sickens the sane man, and hunting the stag is downright barbarous – the first inexcusable on all grounds, the second better done by expert shots with decent guns). The 200 packs of foxhounds kill some 20,000 foxes every season; without those deaths the fox population of approximately 240,000 would, even though the fox is a lazy breeder, rise very fast, and so too would its depredations on the farmer's stock; the farming fraternity could, of course, ameliorate this by giving more room for the hedgerows and copses that shelter the fox's natural prey, but this is an improbable response, and he will take to his shotgun, cyanide and other means of culling this country's largest predator. The fox will be far worse off without the hunt than with it, and may well, like the polecat, be exterminated from all but the fringes of these islands – is this what we want to achieve with the victory of principle?

We shall certainly achieve the virtual extermination of the foxhound. These have been bred to be what they are, and as their genetic and environmental influences, their social isolation in pockets of their own society deprived of petting human contact, will tell for many generations, they are not for taking home to Tooting and sedate walking on a lead, for they will with relish shred your kilims and Laura Ashley curtains, empty their bladders where they will, uproot the hydrangeas in your garden and cause havoc in the street. Heaven forfend that such fine animals should depend on the showman and the breeder for survival and be as corrupted as the poodle, the dachshund and the bulldog – all dogs that once worked for their livings. Do we really want, on grounds of principle, to shoot summarily so many dogs, suddenly useless and impossible to home?

We shall have to slaughter horses too, by the thousand, for without the hunt to follow there will be no purpose in their ownership – perhaps 60,000 of them, decent animals sold for a pittance to dealers who will sell them on abroad to end as steaks in Belgian butchers' shops, or worse, harnessed into slavery for which they are ill-suited. And with the loss of horses, we lose farriers, blacksmiths, saddlers, the whole business of the stable and the point-to-point, and 14,000 now in full-time employ-ment will join the dole queues, their ancient skills, instincts and intuitions fine-honed by experience, utterly useless in any other field. Slaughtered horses and a boost to unemployment – a proper price to pay for principle?

If all these arguments are interpreted as unprincipled casuistry, so be it – they are true. But now let me question the curious priorities of MPs who on grounds of principle put fox-hunting at the top of their list of barbarities to be without delay forbidden. On one side of the balance we have 20,000 foxes torn to shreds by dogs, and on the other we have all the animals we eat; do these meet a more kindly and compassionate death? Did they, indeed, live lives made comfortable by tender husbandry? Were the cows and sheep never abused when sent to market? Let us not forget the report to the Minister of Agriculture last year on the brutal handling of animals in

British markets, so brutal that the bodies of the victims were too bruised for human consumption. How many pigs are driven insane by close confinement in their farrowing and fattening? Consider the battery hen and the bent and broken bones we find in legs and wings, the softness of all the joints that they could barely use in their close-packed lives, and their upside-down deaths on a production line. Consider the upside-down killing of cows and sheep sent by the tens of thousands to their slow and conscious deaths, here in Britain, by Islamic slaughter and the Kosher knife. Consider the brutal business of live animal transport to destinations far abroad. Consider the terrible deaths of fish, dolphins, porpoises and even seals caught in the trawler's net, hauled carelessly from the sea by the compressing ton, the gasping crushed from them. Consider the fish caught for sport by the competitive angler, the hook ripped from the flesh and cartilage, saving a second far more important to the fisherman than the fish's shock and pain – but that's a naughty thought that will lose too many votes. Consider the greed of farmers who, with fertilisers, insecticides and gross industrial methods, poison the earth and destroy the food and habitat of all wild birds and animals.

When such larger issues cry out for remedy, we should have nothing but contempt for MPs who ignore them in favour of the politically correct absurdity of a ban on hunting with the hound. Blinkered and blinded, they support the mooted ban more to save their own pain than that of the fox, their response to the hunt at best a matter of emotion, not of logic, at worst the cynical exploitation of ignorant class prejudice. The hunt must go, and eventually it will; but of its own accord, all that is associated with it slowly accommodated in the decline, its knell hardly noticed at the end. And if cruelty to animals is the true concern of those who would make its end immediate, then let them turn instead to the daily cruelties that know no season's pause in the ports where they will see cows and sheep in transit, let them go to markets and abattoirs where they will see wanton abuse casually enjoyed, let them witness the nightmare horrors inflicted by the halal butcher, and so on, and on. And if it is old-fashioned anthropomorphism that drives MPs to seek to ban the hunt, then let them answer this simple question – would they, in all honesty, prefer to be a battery hen, a veal calf, a bacon pig, a spring lamb, a Norfolk turkey, farmed venison, or a useless horse on its way to Belgium, rather than a fox in the wild working its cunning and its wits to contend with the occasional hazard of the hunt?

If these MPs have any regard for the intelligence of the electorate, they must remedy these larger matters first, and leave the hunt alone.

A GLOSSARY
18 NOVEMBER 1997

For a man in love with the English language – that tough, delicate, elegant and precise instrument of exact understanding – nothing among the annual retrospections of the dying year is more irksome than the list of new words, idioms and phrases that have swept into common parlance and the lexicon. That this year's crop is weak and meagre we must be grateful – negaholic, fluffragette and mezzobrow will not long survive – but those of other years have taken root and flourish on the tongues of teachers, politicians, priests, the good and great. At this moment in time the window of opportunity has not yet closed, and the level playing field is in constant demand. To be at a disadvantage is to lose out (out?), and in this world of intrusive adverbs, John Major, though now sinking in the Waters of Oblivion, will be remembered for signing up to Maastricht – up to? – a double superfluity of adverbs? How could a Prime Minister so murder language? (may Heaven preserve me from a debate on adverbs, particles and prepositions). And with jargon-ridden politicians in our minds, consider spin doctor. Was there ever a more ridiculous term? If we felt compelled to mock the function of the propagandist, then twister, already extant as the man who cheats, confounds, contorts and dissembles, would have been the more accurate and honest word.

A GLOSSARY

I am occasionally rebuked by readers who tell me that my columns cannot be understood without an obsolete dictionary at hand. So be it. I am unrepentant. I take care to ensure that the context offers the general sense of words and phrases that may have become obscure, and that's that – for if we all relinquish our dictionaries when we leave school, our language will grow ever more impoverished. In the spirit engendered by Christmas, however, I offer a brief glossary.

Cacafuego: a boaster and a braggart, or his boasting and his braggartry; from the Latin *cacare*, to void excrement (the origin of words for that activity and the excrement itself from Poland to Portugal – hence cack-handed in English), and the Spanish fuego, fire. Translated literally as shit-fire, it was considered vulgar as early as 1750. To be applied to press releases from the Department of Culture, Media and Sport.

Catamite: from Catamitus, the old Latin form of Ganymede, the beautiful boy carried off by Jupiter to be his cup-bearer and later assumed to have warmed his bed. To be used, in a non-specific sense, of young men who willingly do the bidding of panjandrums (q.v.).

Concubine: a mistress, a cohabiting woman and, occasionally, a woman's male lover; from the Latin *con* and *cubare*, to lie together. Apply as with catamite.

Charabang: from the early 19th century French *char-a-banc*, the first British single-deck motor buses, now known as coaches, were called charabangs, charabancs and charrybongs. The terms survives only in a dismissive and contemptuous sense for use by those who regard coach parties de haut en bas.

Desuetude: a state of decline and disuse, but rich in meaning, suggesting feebleness, even disease; applicable to the Tory Party under John Major.

Ekphrasis: a work of literature inspired by a work of art, or of art by literature – 'a picture is a silent poem, a poem a speaking picture', ran the classical tag - hence Botticelli's supposed Mars and Venus in the National Gallery, based on a text by Aetion, and Keats's 'Ode on a Grecian Urn'; in a satirical sense it may be used of the gush of words let loose when art critics and historians feel compelled to find meaning in works of art promoted by the Serota Tendency (q.v.).

Etiolated: pallid and colourless, as in plants and insects under a stone, and by extension dwarfed, feeble and exhausted, as with much contemporary art and the theology of the Church of England.

Jungible: that which may join or be joined; used of those deemed suitable for membership of the Serota Tendency and the Arts Council, and who may never subsequently become sejungible; not to be confused with Edward Lear's runcible, which applies primarily to bent spoons.

Nabob: an Anglo-Indian corruption of Nawab, the title of a native governor or nobleman, meaning any European who has made great wealth quickly, become accustomed to luxury, and is conspicuous and boastful in his display of both, having been born to neither. It applies to Robert Maxwell and Jeffrey Archer. Its use as an alternative to panjandrum (q.v.) is inaccurate but convenient.

Palimpsest: re-used paper or parchment from which the first script has been incompletely erased, so that its ghostly traces are still visible and even legible; to be used figuratively of a painting on canvas much altered in its development, of an archaeological site with many layers (viz. Troy), or even of ideas, as with the present Labour Government's reflection of past Tory policies.

Panjandrum: a burlesque title for, as the Oxford Dictionary has it, 'a self-constituted high mightiness…or pompous pretender'; to be used

A GLOSSARY

of Cabinet Ministers and local councillors, trustees of museums and opera houses, members of the Arts Council and all other quangos, the great, the good, and the Archbishop of Canterbury. The word was invented in 1754 by the comic dramatist Samuel Foote.

Pelion on Ossa: too much of a good (or bad) thing, not knowing when to stop, and any pointless excess of riches, generous impulses, embarrassments or misfortunes. The image is derived from an episode in Homer's Odyssey when the giants sought to invade Heaven by piling Mount Pelion atop Mount Ossa, and still fell short. To be used of 17th century Dutch paintings of fish and fruit that are beloved of stockbrokers, and of Chancellors' Budgets just before elections.

Phimosis: the tightening of the foreskin so that it cannot be retracted, and thus a word to be used of those with a timorous attitude to great enterprises, and in the context of frustrated aspirations. The condition was suffered by Louis XVI, who failed to sire children until circumcised as an adult, and was of aesthetic appeal to Michelangelo and Eric Gill.

Rima: a conveniently polite word for the genital area of women, from the Latin for fissure, cleft or chink.

Serota Tendency: derived from Militant Tendency, the extreme Left-wing faction of the Labour Party that in the Eighties worked so energetically to infiltrate and subvert the moderate centre, the Serota Tendency has been infinitely more successful in its corruption and command of the visual arts. Serota is not, as one might expect, derived from the Latin sero, to interweave, entwine or bind together, but from the surname of the present director of the Tate Gallery, who has entwined and bound together all the major institutions and instruments of public patronage so that they promote the exhibition of upside-down pianos, dead animals in formaldehyde, and grotesque curiosities devised from ear wax, navel fluff and internal body wastes and fluids. State power and patronage in the contemporary visual arts are now exercised exclusively by his intellectual concubines and catamites.

Shibboleth: a word or sound that betrays a stranger by mispronunciation or incomprehension, as with L and R among the Japanese and the short A of northern England, broadened to become a catchword to the knowing – thus the use of semiotics distinguishes the panjandrums of the Arts Council from occupants of the Clapham omnibus.

Terribilita: from the Latin terribilitas, the English terribility has lapsed into obscurity, but the Italian terribilitd survives in the specific sense of having awe-inspiring quality. Useful in the context of Michelangelo's *Last Judgment*, Verdi's *Requiem*, and any pronouncement by Tony Blair.

Foolish virgins: those who are unprepared, caught short or who have wasted their resources – from Christ's parable of the 10 wise and foolish virgins (Matthew 25. i), five of whom forgot to put oil in their lamps and were thus excluded from the wedding celebrations; applicable to most clients of the Arts Council and all who miss the boat.

The Waters of Oblivion: the image comes from Tales of the Genii published in 1762 as a translation from the Persian, but in fact written by James Ridley, Vicar of Romford. Sadak, an heroic young nobleman is sent by the Sultan to find the Waters of Oblivion; he falls, the waters close over him, and he is lost for ever.

FEBYUREE
27 JANUARY 1998

Feb-yuree is once again upon us and we hear the highly-paid interlocutors and newscasters of radio and television mispronounce the ancient word and deprive it of its origin. We have it from the Romans, whose Februo meant 'I purify by sacrifice', and they in turn had it from the Sabines, who spoke an even older language, of which only a handful of words survive, and for whom February was the time of year when purifying sacrifice was made in preparation for the spring. It then became a Roman festival of purification and Christianity absorbed the ancient practice in the Feast of the Purification of the Virgin Mary.

It would be a pity if late 20th century laziness were to deprive us of 3,000 years of history encapsulated in a single word. We have already lost the verb to februate – to purge or purify – and if February loses its 'r' and it's 'a', it is, as it were, uprooted, and we might as well spell it and speak it any way we choose. This is, of course, the view of those who prate that English is a living language and must be encouraged to change, its constant flux never to be frustrated by academics. The contrary view, however, is that the glory of English is, and has been, the stability of its spelling, its respect for its roots as the source of precise meaning, and the conservative nature of its grammar, syntax, written forms and, in the majority of cases, its pronunciation.

Four centuries ago, as the instrument of a sudden burgeoning of great literature, English stabilised in the forms that we recognise today, but this stability has been steadily eroded over the past 30 years or so. The rot began with those in charge of education in the Sixties, who tended to believe that every local patois, whether it be the mean whine of the South-East or the ugly, adenoidal thickness of the Liverpudlian, was a virtue to be treasured and reflected in local forms of spelling. Old Doctor Johnson preached the reverse when he opined that words are best pronounced as they are spelled, not spelled as they are pronounced. One consequence of such compliant teaching is that now, decades later, most members of the profession can neither speak nor spell with clarity and accuracy, and the idea of a received English that all can understand has been abandoned.

In this we serve ourselves badly, but we serve our immigrant communities far worse; it is cruel to have inflicted the ugly brogues of Birmingham and Bradford on Indians and Pakistanis who, had they been educated in the sub-continent, would have learned to speak less obscurely accented English and a more classical vocabulary; it is cruel that Afro-Caribbeans have exchanged the fluency of language in the West Indies, enriched by many alien sources, for the impoverished inarticulacy of Brixton.

No one in his senses will argue for a single unaccented homogeneity of speech throughout the length and breadth of Britain, for that is not the alternative to pockets of regional patois so strong that their speakers are to all intents and purposes incomprehensible to neighbours across the county boundary, but we must acknowledge that extremes of accent that bear scant resemblance to the written forms of English are a barrier to literacy, particularly for the poorest and most deprived in our society. Ever more stress is placed on literacy by our political masters – and quite rightly – but when we reach the point at which the geography and history to which literacy is the open sesame, must be sacrificed in order to give more time to the reading and writing in which schoolchildren are so weak, things have come to a pretty pass.

Perhaps dictation is no longer a teaching exercise – and if that is so, more's the pity, for it compelled the teacher to speak with clarity of phrasing and not to elide the consonants, and it compelled children to listen and translate sounds into literary symbols. Dictation led to better spelling, better diction, better phrasing and a feeling for interval and the rhythmic rise and fall of speech. This brings us back to Febyuree. How is a child to spell it if his teacher speaks it so? What is he to make of Jan-yuree, deteriate, secertary and even eddicate? How should he spell sure when our three times educated Prime Minister invariably says shewer?

Teachers alone are not to blame – many are as much the victims of political correctitude as their pupils in this fervent support of local accents as a cultural right, and in the silly business of the he or she, the his or hers, and all the other gender nonsenses that now confuse the flow of English. We must take into account the seemingly irresistible invasion of pseudo-technical and computer languages, the pseudo-American and gutter-English affectations of pop and rock singers, and the tendency of all to turn nouns into verbs – accessing, authorising (writing), trialling and so on. Our political masters know not what they say – refute for rebut, militate for mitigate, importantly for important, infer for imply, this last so common that grammarians have surrendered to the error, though the difference is clear and one infers or understands from an implication. But why should one expect better from our politicians when a professor of English, broadcasting on the BBC, utters such an infelicity as 'these kind of changes'.

The BBC, too, must shoulder blame. No institution has greater power to support the beauty and majesty of English, yet neglects its duty more. Those it employs to write for announcers and newsreaders care not a hoot for grammar or clear meaning, and make elementary errors of construction; and those who read them often have the accents of far provincial slums. Poetry on Radio 4 is in the hands of Ian McMillan and Simon Armitage, poor speakers laden with dreary northern tones. Children's television is dominated by yelling loutish youngsters with the language of the streets. Late evening discussions for adults that once brought us wisdom and insight now bring us Robert Elms, a young man whose English is Wapping argot – and we must have no doubt that were he not so cockney, the BBC would not offer him employment. Anyone who has any doubt about the 'dumbing down' of John Birt's Corporation will find it resolved by the infantile Robert and his it's Later Than You Think.

It is indeed later than we think, and the worthy Education Secretary David Blunkett's near panic over reading, writing and arithmetic is wholly justified. The BBC, publicly funded and with a responsibility to public service, could be his greatest ally in a campaign that is now desperately urgent, but he is betrayed by John Birt, the enemy of educated English, a Feb-yuree man.

TURKEY IN EUROPE
3 FEBRUARY 1998

When the second millennium dawned, Catholic Rome was in the ascendant as the heart of Christianity and Orthodox Byzantium was in decline and on the point of losing the Holy Places to Islam – the Seljuk Turks took Jerusalem in 1071. Their recovery became the objective of the first Crusade in 1096, and in the following centuries Byzantium was so ravaged, despoiled, enfeebled and reduced by Christians from the west that she could not resist the long, slow and inexorable invasion of the Turks from central Asia. With the fall of Constantinople in 1453, the great city that for 1,100 years had borne the name of Rome's first Christian Emperor became the capital of the Ottoman Empire, an Islamic power that was to reach from the walls of Vienna to the Yemen, from Morocco to the Caspian Sea.

For most of the second millennium, the Turks have been a major factor in European politics, secular and religious, always as the destroyer and the enemy, never the friend, always menacing, even in their 19th century decline and decadence. Byron, fighting for Greek independence, taught us to hate Johnny Turk, and politicians to fear him as the instrument of a route to India from Germany or Russia. We watched, even encouraged, the total ethnic cleansing of Crete between 1896 and 1907 as the Muslims were expelled to the southern shores of Turkey. We settled, here in London, the terms of the first Balkan war in 1913, reducing Turkey's possessions in Europe to a tiny toehold west of Istanbul, and then watched in dismay as within weeks these borders were redrawn in the second Balkan war, Turkey regaining most of Thrace. With the outbreak of the First World War, Turkey a German ally, Lawrence of Arabia preached Byron's gospel to the Arabs and became an even more romantic hero; at its end, Turkey's borders were redrawn yet again and she was much reduced. In the east Iraq was invented by the British to gain control of oilfields at Mosul; in the west the British, French and Greeks took as much as they could from her Mediterranean holdings, the Greeks even from mainland Anatolia; and thus were sown the seeds of unremitting enmity in the Aegean, and of unremitting revolt with the western powers' refusal to acknowledge the rights of Kurds to a homeland of their own.

We live with these problems still, and they affect our response to Turkey's application to join the European Union. Turkey is angry that all the nations that for half a century have been compliant dominions of Russian communism now have hopes of joining the EU, but she, though signatory to an association with the EEC in 1963, an applicant for membership in 1987, and in Customs Union with the EU since 1996, has been refused an invitation. Turkey has long been a member of Nato and the Council of Europe; she has been the West's bulwark against Russian expansion in that quarter since the Second World War; she was, and still is, our ally against Saddam Hussein since the war over Kuwait, and cutting off the Iraqi oil pipeline has cost her dear – perhaps as much as $10 billion a year in revenues. Now, as a secular state with a largely Muslim population, she has a new significance as a western bastion against politically militant Islam.

TURKEY IN EUROPE

We owe Turkey a great deal for her collaboration since the last war, but the pseudo-Christian propaganda of a thousand years lurks in our folk memory, and we find it convenient to blackball her membership of our European Club because her armies occupy almost half of Cyprus and are engaged in a cruel war of national suppression against the Kurds who populate her eastern provinces.

Cyprus – where many a British soldier was maimed or murdered by Greeks in the name of their proposed union with Greece, the minority Turkish Cypriots then our allies (more or less) – is a welcomed candidate for the EU, and the Turkish army must depart, we argue. But if we have forgotten what the Greeks did to the Turks in Crete when they cleared the island of them 100 years ago, the Turks have not.

As for the Kurds, a nation native to eastern Turkey (which the Turks are not), their homeland and history as ancient as the Hittites, their language Chaldean, Babylonian and of pre-biblical antiquity – it is we, the British, who thought this nomadic and tribal people of no account when we determined the borders of Turkey, Persia and Iraq; we, the British, who failed to foresee and prevent a problem that now ruins Turkey's reputation as a democratic country fit to be our equal in the European Union.

On these two rocks is wrecked the Turks' ambition to be European, to the great glee of the Greeks, their undying enemies since a million of them were murdered in or driven out of Izmir and its hinterland in 1922-24. And there are other reasons for not admitting the Turks – their inflation, which has forced the rate of exchange from 30 lira to the pound in 1975 to more than 340,000 in 1998, their rapidly rising uncontrolled birthrate, unemployment, figures that cannot be measured, and poverty of almost Indian quality. But above all these reasons one more is most important – if the European Union expands too far, it will falter and fan. The history of Europe is one of short-lived empires; Rome could not hold it, nor Charlemagne's heirs, nor any Holy Roman Emperor, nor Austria, nor Napoleon, nor Hitler, nor, for all her tanks and armies, lackeys and satraps, indoctrination and impious philosophy, could Russia.

The Union, with 15 members, is already absurdly overextended, but with a bit more give and take it has some small chance of finding a modus vivendi in its present form. If, however, we extend it from Portugal to the Pripet Marshes, and from Britain to Bessarabia, which is what we seriously propose, or from Donegal to Dogubayazit as the Turks wish, we condemn it to bankruptcy and fragmentation in far less time than it took the restlessness of nations to undo the work of tyrants in the past. Those sceptics who relish the confounding of the EU should, of course, welcome Bulgaria, Latvia, Estonia, Slovenia and all the others of the dozen Ruritanian aspirants, and preach most favourably of all for Turkey's membership.

EASTER
7 APRIL 1998

The agnostic who was once a devout and observant Christian can take Christmas in his stride as no more than an ancient fairy-tale, or the happy business of the pantomime, embroidered with the panoply of kings, the wide-eyed wonder of unwashed shepherds, and the innocent wisdom of an ass and ox. Easter, however, may still trouble him, tugging at his conscience even though decades have passed since his last genuflexion, his last presence at a Mass, for at Easter, the saintly man who some 2,000 years ago preached the Beatitudes, and in these blessings of Christian perfection laid the foundations of the compassionate society – 'Blessed are the merciful...the peacemakers...the persecuted...ye are the salt of the earth...ye are the light of the world...' – was betrayed, put to death, and buried in a tomb.

It was no ordinary betrayal, but the worst of treacheries – that of a friend, a seemingly fond kiss its signal. It was no ordinary death; this was a man who stood before the Roman Governor of Judaea and, in his refusal to deny that he was the King of the Jews, brought upon himself the spiteful degradation of the extreme punishment reserved for slaves – crucifixion, and its inevitable preliminary, scourging, the Crown of Thorns an exquisite refinement. It was no ordinary burial; this was a body that had hung for hours naked in the spring sunshine and then in the chill of sudden darkness, that had trembled uncontrollably with the shock of terrible wounds, of which every joint and tendon had been stretched beyond endurance, choking every time the head fell forward, utter exhaustion the last mercy; yet this was the body that flung aside its linen grave cloths and was resurrected from the dead.

Perhaps this was all true in some literal sense. We can accept the betrayal without a moment's hesitation, for we have all been the recipients and givers of the traitor's kiss. We can accept that a brave and principled man might well have stood his ground before a Governor, for many have done so, both before and since, and met their deaths for it. We can even argue that Christ was not dead when taken from the cross, that deep coma had saved him from the soldiers sent to break his legs and hasten death, that in the quiet grave he recovered enough to make his escape, and that the business of angels and the sepulchre's rolling stone were the embroideries of those who should have guarded him instead of sleeping, exactly as recorded at the end of Matthew's Gospel.

But no matter how logically, reasonably, possibly and probably we interpret the tale, we are left with a misgiving, for the Roman witnesses of Christ's Crucifixion, those who had no Jewish axe to grind but were merely Caesar's more-than-my-job's-worth boys, doing their duty, carrying out instructions, were inclined to say, 'Certainly, this was a righteous man,' and, 'Truly, this man was the Son of God.' Christ's death is tellingly remembered in the Roman Catholic office of Tenebrae (occasionally adopted by Puseyite clerics in the Church of England too), performed more or less continuously from Good Friday until Easter Sunday as a recollection of the darkness that blotted out the sun while Christ was hanging on the cross, and of the three days that he was lying in his tomb. Tenebrae is the most disturbing and convincing service in the Liturgy –

EASTER

or perhaps was, for it is just the kind of office that a Church, seeking to make the practices of its faith more comfortable and accessible, might discard to save its congregation's aching knees. It is poetic, theatrical and terrible; its very name means darkness, and the windows of the church are draped in black, the images muffled, the altars closed. On or before the altar, arranged in a pyramid, stand 13 flaming candles of the pure beeswax that is a symbol of Christ's virginity (bees were long believed, like fish, the earliest of Christian symbols, to be sexless); one by one, after the singing of each penitential psalm, these are extinguished until only the central light is left, and this is carried behind the altar as a symbol of Christ's burial. Early on Easter Day the great columnar Paschal Candle is lit, and from its flame all other candles take their fire, until the following Tenebrae.

This arduous service has a mystical beauty, touches the emotions, and in some small way compels the man on his knees into closer communion with Christ than at any other time in the Christian calendar. Is this belief? Or is it mere empathy – the identification with the performer that is felt by the spectator at an opera or tragedy, the emotional response to great painting or great literature? If the Church has dispensed with Tenebrae ('Such an inaccessible word, nowadays; Latin, you know – really rather elitist'), then the Church is an ass. But then the Church is an ass, for in dispensing with so many of its mysteries, particularly in its descent into today's vernacular, it encourages disbelief and even resentment that its priests can take their congregations for gullible fools. I went to Mass last Christmas for the first time for many years and, enthralled by the exultant music, felt my agnosticism threatened – could there still be in me, sceptic, cynic, unrepentant sinner, some dormant seed of trust and faith? The question lay in my mind only until the first words of the sermon, and then: I was the beneficiary of such insulting, patronising, puerile bilge that it was all I could do to stay in my seat, the seduction of the music quite undone.

Priests, I suspect, should keep silence. They may be necessary instruments of God, but the banality of their exhortations undoes the beauty of ancient ritual and text, and their inability to answer questions with anything other than hack platitudes undoes their intellectual status. And not just the priests of Rome: Thought for the Day is part of my daily listening, and it exposes me to the housewife drivel of the Church of England's women priests, to the babble and blather of the non-conformist Welshman and dissenting Scot, and to the incomprehensible ravings of the protestant Ulsterman. The Archbishop of Canterbury, on Easter Day last year, spoke for all of them when he preached of God's 'deep love for his creation and his desire that we should experience the fullness of that love'. The fullness of that love? Love as demonstrated in Bosnia, Rwanda and Angola? As in the refugee camps of Malaysia and Thailand? As in the prisons of Red China? As in the repression of East Timor and Tibet? As in the burning forests of Brazil? As in Dunblane and Lockerbie? As in the multitude of daily miseries that never make the news? And above all as in the attitude of God's chosen people to those of Palestine?

Blessed are the merciful, the peacemakers and the persecuted. Yes, indeed and indeed – but what has the spiteful, careless, mocking God we know from everyday experience to do with these? Jesus Christ makes better sense as a mere man than as the son of such a fickle monster, and Christianity as a profound political philosophy than as a superstition requiring belief.

ENOCH POWELL
21 APRIL 1998

The art of oratory is dead. Repartee survives, and the snappy soundbite – that thoroughly nasty infestation of the Nineties – flourishes, but the quiet and slow first words, then their increasing pace, the shortening interval between the phrases, the strengthening tone, and at last, adrenaline and imagination crowding the brain, the crescendo of idea and voice – all these have gone to join the Dodo. More than half a century since Winston Churchill whipped us into patriotic fervour with his undoubting declarations that we would fight the Nazis on our beaches, expending blood, sweat, toil and tears, mimics mimicking mimics still amuse us with their mimicry – but who among them, or among us, for that matter, could quote with absolute certitude the lapidary English of 'Never in the field of human conflict was so much owed by so many to so few,' or rehearse the argument that leads inexorably to the perfection of that Ciceronian sentiment?

Since then, how little we recall of oratory – Macmillan's wind of change, perhaps, the pound in Harold Wilson's pocket remembered as a classic of deceit, and Mrs Thatcher's 'No, no, no', but apart from these only one other 20th century voice still echoes – a thin voice pitched high in the uneasy intonation of his native Black Country, the voice of Enoch Powell quoting Virgil to a few Conservative worthies in Birmingham on 20

65

April 1968. One may ponder for a moment the folly of wasting the words of Virgil on such an audience: one may assert that had he left it in the original Latin, none would have known its relevance; and one may suggest that Virgil expressed other sentiments more suited to such an audience – 'Where the Briton stands, utterly estranged from all the world', or, of Britain, 'While the rivers run to the ocean…and the sky shall nourish the stars, always shall thy honour, thy name and thy glory abide', but he chose to offer them, as though it ran through Wolverhampton, the constituency for which he was MP, 'the River Tiber, foaming with much blood'.

Powell might as well at once have emulated Seneca and committed suicide, as did that antique philosopher at the behest of Nero for supposed treachery, for Edward Heath, his Nero, demanded his immediate resignation from the Shadow Cabinet and put an end to his career as a significant politician. Thirty years on, this 'River of Blood Speech', as it was dubbed, is now almost all that we know of Powell, and its sentiments have been so distorted, falsified and perverted that we have come to believe them to be those of one driven by so rabid a prejudice against men of different race and colour that he urged his audience to commit monstrous deeds of slaughter. He did nothing of the kind, but into the last paragraph of the speech, the summing-up of unremarkable misgivings about the Race Relations Bill shared with many of his peers, he slipped the sentence 'Like the Roman, I seem to see the River Tiber, foaming with much blood'. The preceding sentence was 'As I look ahead, I am filled with foreboding', and the following sentence was a clear reference to the murder of Martin Luther King that had occurred only 16 days before – 'That tragic and intractable phenomenon which we watch with horror on the other side of the Atlantic…' Whose blood then was it that he saw foaming in the Wolverhampton Tiber? It was the blood of Negroes (for it was then still possible to use this now execrated word), spilled by the Wolverhampton equivalent of the Ku Klux Klan, and far from inciting aggression against the Afro-Caribbeans, he sought to warn them against impending violence.

The speech is an example of the cool undiplomatic logic that was characteristic of Powell, saying what he believed must be said, clearly and without dissembling, without duplicity, drawing nothing from the politicians' over flowing font of sanctimonious abstractions – the avoidable evils of the future were for him the necessary occupation of the politician and not to be shirked. Alas, he chose to make his observations on immigration to a small and by no means classically educated group of Brummies incapable of understanding his customary oratory. He was compelled to lower his intellectual sights and to employ the easy and familiar device of anecdote, the little old lady as the sole surviving white much troubled in an inner-city area colonised by self-concerned black immigrants; it was corny and beneath him, but effective with this particular audience when arguing for tight controls on immigration, 'by stopping further inflow…and by promoting the maximum outflow.' We forget, and so did Edward Heath at the time, that this was official Conservative policy; Mrs Thatcher did not forget it, and advised Heath to hold back from dismissing Powell, saying that his was 'a conclusion jumped too far, too rapidly'.

And there's the rub. Before we too jump too far, or unquestioningly comply with the anathema pronounced on Powell, we should look back full 30 years, at the intellectual and political climate of the day, at the early growths of political correctitude, at the first signs of what Powell then described as 'the one-way privilege' of the minorities now so familiar and irksome to the rest of us, and at the use of an Act of Parliament to remove the legal right to express opposition to that privilege. We have only to recall the Islamic hullaballoo over Salman Rushdie's *Satanic Verses* to see how right Powell was when he spoke of the immigrants' 'vested interests in the preservation and sharpening of racial differences'. Powell was a racist only in the sense that he believed race to be the root of every man's identity; he believed profoundly in cultural difference, not in cultural inferiority; he had nothing but contempt for the multiculturalism that has now developed into the meaningless intellectual sludge in which all our cultures are submerged, for he believed that cultural integration brought far greater loss than gain. That he was not a racist in any conventional sense is evident to anyone who cares to consult his courageous philippic against the Conservative government in 1959, when 11 half-starved Mau-Mau prisoners of the Kenyan authorities directly responsible to the Colonial Secretary were bludgeoned to death by their warders for refusing to undertake slave labour; the risk of sacrifice to which he then exposed his political career was brave indeed, and for a few black men who had violently and murderously opposed white rule, far away from Wolverhampton, easily dismissed as savages – but Powell was a man who believed in human rights and in the value of other men's cultures as much as his own.

But there's the other rub – what was Powell's culture? He was a lower- middle-class romantic of professorial bent, rooted equally in the classical past of ancient Greece and Rome, their glory and their grandeur, and in the ideal England of Shrop-shire lads and larks ascending, of Elgar's Nimrod and Hardy's Wessex, and of a British Empire that across the world spread Christianity, medicine and equality under the law. He seemed not to recognise that this English dream had been destroyed by the 1914-18 war long before he grew into long trousers, and that the concepts of honour, nobility, sacrifice, virtue and gravity beyond the ordinary limits of human endeavour, though they made him a man of unbending principle, no longer applied in public life and merely puzzled the pragmatic politicians all around him.

Bookish, men said of him, 'driven mad by the remorselessness of his own logic' – yet this was a man who spoke for Homosexual Law Reform, and against the death penalty, long before liberalism in these matters became fashionable, and could be (and was, visibly) deeply moved by poetry, particularly by the words of A E Housman, his Latin professor at Cambridge. Housman, far more than Cicero and Seneca, formed him; it was Housman, speaking through him, as it were, who said for Powell: 'I wish I had been killed in the war,' forming his imagination with such lines as 'The lads that will die in their glory and never be old', and 'By brooks too broad for leaping, the lightfoot boys are laid'. Powell was born 20 years too late – the First World War, the Great, not the Second, was the war for him, when loyalty to Empire and England inspired the men who willingly went to it, believing in green fields and even Wolverhampton.

Powell's Birmingham speech of April 1968, pruned of the oratorical touches of Virgilian vision and the tale of the marooned old lady, though it remains perceptive and prescient, is not the least inflammatory, but merely a dull rehearsal of Conservative policy, its only virtue that it is bluntly to the point; even with the vision and the dame, Michael Foot, later Leader of the Labour Party, could see nothing racist in it. Before we join the chorus of damnation that still echoes after 30 years, we should read the speech and understand exactly what Powell said.

THE ELGIN MARBLES
12 MAY 1998

Some 15 years have passed since Miss Melina Mercouri first pleaded in her tobacco-ravaged voice for the return to Greece of the Elgin Marbles. Strong men melted and succumbed to her seduction, and if anyone could have secured the restoration of the Marbles to the Parthenon, it was she with her campaigning zeal, flashing eyes and antique histrionics – but she failed, and now that she has gone to join the Muses on Parnassus the argument too should die and not rumble on, as it does, with occasional eruptions of spite and enmity.

Athens has managed very well without the Marbles since Lord Elgin rescued them in the first quinquennium of the 19th century. The Turks, whose Ottoman Empire then embraced all Greece and most of the Balkans, paid them scant regard, occasionally knocking off their vulnerable part for sport or to oblige passing travellers with souvenirs, but the Greeks themselves did far worse damage by grinding them down for mortar. Witnessing this, Elgin felt it his duty to save them from further depredation, applied to the Turkish Government for permission to excavate and remove what he thought he should, and receive of a permit instructing the local governor not to molest him, nor to hinder him 'from taking away any pieces of stone with inscriptions or figures…' At his own expense – £74,240 – Elgin sent most of the Marbles to London, where in

1816 the Government bought them for £35,000, forcing Elgin, deep in debt, to flee to France, where he died.

In London the Marbles entered the history of western art. A few envious souls dismissed them, but most sculptors and painters were enthusiastic, Flaxman, Haydon, Wilkie, West, Lawrence, Fuseli, Nollekins, Westmacott and Chantrey among them – thus the loftiest academicians and artists old and young supported Elgin, and when Canova (he of the Three Graces in the V&A) came to London in 1815 his disinterested praise was overwhelming – 'Oh to unlearn all that I have learned – at last I see what ought to form the real school of sculpture.' Carved between 447 and 440 BC, for some 2,000 years these sculptures had been ignored, until Elgin's efforts and expenditure gave them new life and influence.

Suppose he had left them where they lay, fallen from their original high position in the Parthenon partly in the 5th century AD, when the building was converted to a Christian church (zealous Christians were then responsible for much defacement of the sculptures), and partly in 1687 when the Turks were using it as a powder magazine and a Venetian shell scored a direct hit on it, what then? – the Turks and the native Greeks would have continued their piecemeal destruction. When the Greeks achieved independence from the Turks, they cared so little for their classical heritage that they proposed to demolish and remodel the Acropolis as a palace for their first king, Otto of Bavaria, and designs were prepared by Schinkel, the greatest of German architects, in 1834.

But who were these Greeks, early in the 19th century, and who are they now? They are not the Greeks of the ancient pre-Christian city societies that still capture the imaginations of all educated, romantic, oppressed and hopeful people who dream of democracy.

They are not the Greeks whose language, literature and philosophies have formed the course of culture in the western world these past 2,000 years. These are not the Greeks whose art and architecture, pillaged by the ancient Romans and carried off to Italy, eventually gave birth to the glories of the Italian Renaissance. Ancient Greece, the mother of us all, subsided into a feeble, superstition-ridden, near-pagan agrarian society with not an idea in its head, its stock corrupted by Saracens, Sicilians, Normans, Bulgars, Venetians, Turks and any old Levantine, and I dare say that even the Scandinavian Varangians on their way to guard Byzantium planted a flaxen seed or two. Put so, the hereditary right to the Marbles lies anywhere from Reykjavik to Alexandria as much as to the mongrel race that has inherited Thessaly and Attica.

And what use, since the Turks acknowledged the independence of Greece in 1829, has this mongrel race made of the substantial classical remains not removed by Lord Elgin? Has there been in the best part of two centuries the slightest evidence of a cultural revival? Who among us can name one single Greek painter, sculptor or architect of any interest at all, let alone one whose work can be interpreted as a continuity of the noble past to which they lay false claim? Take one look at Athens now and we see a city over which Pericles would weep, graceless, ugly, squalid and polluted, a monument to 20th century greed and exploitation owing nothing to Callimachus and Praxiteles.

We should treat the Greek claim to the Elgin Marbles with contempt, not only because their argument of cultural continuity is spurious, but because to demand the return of museum objects to their countries of origin is a menacing absurdity to the museum concept that has done so much to preserve and advance the many cultures of the world. The

THE ELGIN MARBLES

Marbles have played their part in European culture precisely because they have been in the British Museum and not rotting in the mephitic air of Athens, just as – our own little local difficulty – the Lindisfarne Gospels have been held in awe and wonder by millions who could never have seen them shut in the Schatzkammer of Durham Cathedral or some other prison of the north.

The inexorable logic of the Athens argument is that all the Mesopotamian treasures in the British Museum should be sent to Iraq, all the Venetian masterpieces in the National Gallery to Venice, the Wallace Collection's *Laughing Cavalier* to Holland and, Heaven forefend, that all the paintings everywhere by Turner should come back to London. This implies the destruction of the British Museum, the Louvre and the great museums of Berlin, Leningrad and New York, cultural impoverishment the inevitable consequence.

One must argue that antique Roman sculpture would have been the poorer had Sulla and others not robbed Greece and transported treasures back to Rome, that Neo-Classicism could not have burgeoned all over Europe had not Rome trafficked in her past, that our passionate respect for Benin bronzes was engendered entirely by our pillaging them less than a century ago, and that the diligent care given such objects by museums has been a marvellous aid to scholarship and connoisseurship as well as to the judicious intermingling of cultural influences.

To return the Elgin Marbles to Athens would be a precedent the only consequence of which would be cultural disaster. It must never be allowed to happen.

AKIHITO'S GARTER
19 MAY 1998

There are in the Imperial War Museum some drawings by Ronald Searle, the inventor of that preposterous school for girls, St Trinian's. They have nothing to do with dark blue knickers, gym slips and jolly hockey sticks, but are instead Searle's witness to the particularly nasty war in which, as a very young man, he fought and was for three years a prisoner. This was the war in Singapore and Burma in which the Japanese, that ancient people of exquisite civilisation and culture, treated their British prisoners in much the same way as the Germans treated gypsies, Jews, Slavs and homosexuals in their concentration camps – with cold continuous cruelty, fired by sadism.

In Auschwitz, Dachau and Belsen there are regretful memorials of German inhumanity, and on suitable occasions these old enemies have the good grace to draw attention to their guilt and offer grudging remedy. The clever Japanese, however, have turned things topsy-turvy, so that of the Far Eastern campaigns we remember, above all, the atom bomb on Hiroshima, so that it is we who have assumed the guilt, while the horrors of their work and death camps are forgotten, but for occasional revivals of *The Bridge over the River Kwai* and the derring-do of well-fed film stars. There are no Japanese memorials to the men whom, against all the Conventions of Geneva, they starved and beat and worked to death as in their oriental beastliness, their callous disregard for western sensibilities and their brutal scorn for the vanquished, they built the Burma-Siam Railway at the cost of 120,000 human lives – 462 deaths for each mile of track, a corpse every four yards.

When, on 15 February 1942, Singapore capitulated to the Japanese, terrible consequences followed: some 20,000 Chinese civilians, and perhaps as many more Malays, were shot or beheaded, their bodies left to rot in the streets, their heads spiked on poles or displayed on rough shelves at table height to warn others against underground activities or attempts to feed the British prisoners whose steady, unremitting degradation Searle recorded. Malnutrition, tropical ulcers, malaria and cholera took their toll as his subjects deteriorated from scrawny to skeletal, their eyes first blank, then hollow. In a study of a man dying of cholera, propped against a pole, death rattling in his throat, the thin lines of the draughtsman match the Belsen-like emaciation; other dying men turn from the light like old dogs. These were soldiers in whom the Japanese recognised no honour; they were despised shameful captives, some compelled to wear armbands identifying them as fit for sport by their captors, the legend reading 'One who has been captured in battle and is to be beheaded or castrated at the will of the Emperor.'

That Emperor was Hirohito. His son Akihito is about to make state visit to this country with, no doubt, all the business of gold-plated dinners and carriage rides along The Mall. These we must accept as the necessary nonsense of tradition, the pantomime accorded to every Ruritanian despot and African dictator, but for Akihito there is to be in addition the exceptional honour that the Queen is to dub him an Extra Knight of the Garter. The Most Noble Order of the Garter is our highest order of chivalry, limited to the Sovereign in whose gift it is and to 25 knights of the Sovereign's choosing; to these may occasionally be added members of foreign royal families. It is an ancient order, the 650th anniversary of its foundation to be celebrated this year. As an order of chivalry it should be worn only by the chivalrous – a word that describes the perfect knight, a man of disinterested bravery, honour and courtesy, a man who is gallant and magnanimous in victory, a man who in some residual sense lives his life in accordance with codes religious, moral and social that reach as far into the past as the Arthurian legends. Akihito is so clearly not such a man that to award him the Garter is to diminish all who already wear its habits and insignia.

How has this insult come about? Is this most revered of honours to be given to Akihito because he has asked for it in exchange for his ludicrous equivalent – a Johnny-come-lately of diplomatic baubles called The Supreme Order of the Chrysanthemum? Is it to be given him as a commercial bribe because to our new young Prime Minister the war was a long time ago and in a place remote, fought by men who are now old and dying and of no use or value to him in his Cool Britannia? Is the Garter now so devalued that it is to be awarded on mere precedent and so as not to offend a man whose father and grandfather were given it?

If the Queen and the Prime Minister gather at the Cenotaph each raw November to honour the dead of two World Wars, how can they consider, even for one moment, the gift of our Most Noble Order to the Sovereign of a nation that has not the slightest notion of chivalry in a western sense? Whose honour is at stake in this matter? – the honour of the 120,000 men who died on that damned railway, and all the other allied soldiers throughout the vast spread of campaigns in the Far East and the Pacific Ocean who were killed, captured, tortured and slaughtered for sport and convenience? – or the honour of a puppet emperor here only for the further economic benefit of Tokyo? When next we buy our poppies of remembrance, we should remember just how ignoble were our Japanese enemies.

The ageing body of men who survived Japanese imprisonment, slavery and torture have every right to demonstrate when Akihito is here. His ministers have consistently refused to see or talk to them, his father offered no apology, and the only compensation has been the insulting trifle fixed long ago before American investment and relief from the costs of their defence gave the Japanese so powerful a boost that theirs became the world's most successful economy. We should support the prisoners in their protest, for if this Emperor feels insulted, he has only himself to blame. An honourable man would long ago have apologised on behalf of his nation and then made suitable amends. Old enemies could then have been reconciled.

Look again at the drawings in the Imperial War Museum, at the starving prisoner holding a rock above his head as a Japanese guard teases him with a kick and the prick of a bayonet in his back, at a beaten prisoner carried away unconscious, at more deaths and more brutalities, and at the tender studies of three kittens that on Christmas Day 1944 Searle and his friends 'gently fried…a memorable meal…delicate…delectable.' Think of such things when Akihito kowtows to the Queen and gets his Garter.

RITUAL SLAUGHTER
7 JULY 1998

One of the more engaging snippets of news last week was that Dr Mo Mowlam had entertained the bureaucrats of Brussels to a feast of British beef. As the export ban on beef from Northern Ireland is about to be lifted, what more suitable celebration could there have been than the sight of the Secretary of State at the head of a great table as the barons, topsides, tournedos, sirloins and Chateaubriands were borne in on which the assembled ministers, diplomats, civil servants, vets, scientists and farmers were to gorge? Think of it in terms of a painting by old Pieter Brueghel, who was born nearby – the faces ruddy and sweating with gluttony as fine red wines, sizzling fat, succulent flesh and bloody gravy took their toll on decorum, as the paper hats emerged from crackers and the speech of speeches slurred, as farmers in their clod-hop boots took to the table top and danced a merry jig.

There cannot have been a farmer in the whole of the United Kingdom who was not, in spirit, with Dr Mowlam and her guests – but what about the bullocks, cows and calves? Are we to see the resurgence of the live animal export trade as the consequence of the decline of BSE and relief from the ban on exports?

There can be no doubt in our minds that the transport of farm animals over long distances causes them serious distress, and the longer the journey the more animals are injured and the more die in transit, crushed, stifled and trampled to death in overcrowded lorries, or so terrified that fear puts an end to them. There are such deaths and injuries within the British Isles, but there are many more on trans-European journeys, and more still among animals shipped to the Near East.

The Southern Irish send vast numbers of cattle to the Near East – out into the wild Atlantic, left between the Pillars of Hercules, and then the length of the Mediterranean Sea, past Sardinia and Sicily, south of Crete and Cyprus, to a wretched landing in the Lebanon or Syria. Storms cause terrible injuries, and animals arrive with broken legs and backs, incapable of being driven from the ships; these, chained by whatever extremity is handy, are unloaded by crane and roughly dumped on the quay, compounding their injuries, and some slip from their chains and fall many feet. And there they lie for many hours until some slaughterman takes them as a perk.

Slaughterman? The term suggests some element of skill, but all that is required in a Muslim abattoir is the brutal ability to beat or wrestle an animal to the ground and then slit its throat. Twenty-four years ago, when I first saw Muslims slaughter a cow, it was still the ritual business of crating the terrified animal and turning it to hang head down before the knife was drawn across the throat and the belly simultaneously slit to let the intestines tumble out, and it took what seemed an age to die in the great spread of blood and guts. That was bad enough, but with the passage of 20 years the improved standard of living has made meat much more prominent in the Near Eastern diet, and conditions for animals in abattoirs have worsened by far with the demand for quantity.

They wait on floors slippery with faeces, watching what happens in the slaughter area, and are then dragged by ropes and their own tails, or beaten with iron bars, to get them near the drains into which their blood must flow; there, boys and men kick their legs from under them, jump on their backs – anything to make them fall so that their heads can be held back – and in this state of terror their throats are cut, more or less.

If more, then death is fairly swift – a minute or so of struggling to get to their feet, and then consciousness is gone; if less, then the loss of blood is slow and for as much as two or three minutes the bull or cow will make frantic efforts to stand, and then, too weak, succumb to the dreadful business of drowning in its own blood – perhaps five minutes in all. It is evident that these brutal procedures brutalise those who inflict them. It is evident that the younger boys find the abattoir a place of fun – yes, fun – and that vindictive acts of cruelty excite them to do more.

What has any of this to do with Mo Mowlam's merry luncheon? The probability that cattle reared in the verdant pastures of her Six Counties will now join the export trade from Lire, and will suffer this appalling fate, and that when the beef ban is lifted from the whole of the Kingdom, animals from every part of it will be exported for such slaughter. I am not a vegetarian. I recognise from my appetite for meat that I am as much a carnivore as any man, but I have, to a very large extent, abandoned it as part of my diet, for my respect for animals is such that I believe in better husbandry than this. This leads me to the perilous subject of so-called ritual slaughter in this country – the halal of Muslims and the shechita of Jews – perilous as anyone rash enough to criticise the practices of these minorities is inevitably accused of racial prejudice. Both methods involve the bleeding to death of the fully conscious animal. All slaughtered animals bleed to death, but in licensed abattoirs they are stunned and deeply unconscious before their throats are cut. It is hardly a method that we would choose for dispatching human beings – and in that context I doubt if we would describe it as humane – but it is significantly less cruel and less prolonged than halal slaughter; it is, moreover, better supervised.

The Ministry of Agriculture exercises little, if any, supervision over ritual killing for the Muslim and Jewish communities. Anecdotal evidence suggests that a shochet, a Jewish slaughterman undergoes rigorous training and is unlikely to be careless or deliberately cruel; there is, however, irrefutable evidence that Muslim slaughtermen in Britain lack training and skill, and are unsupervised. The Muslim fraternity also practises private slaughter – I have witnessed the slaughter of sheep at the site on which a new house was to be built; it is illegal here, and is contrary to a European Directive (No 95/119/EC) but it is nevertheless common wherever Muslims live. Many readers will recall reports of the Parisian killing field in which French Muslims slaughtered hundreds of animals on the Feast of Sacrifices, 'a scene more fitting to the Dark Ages…to turn the hardiest stomach', as the *Daily Mail*'s man put it last year.

The Conservatives were terrified of confronting halal slaughter, maintaining it to be 'a fundamental matter of religious belief to communities who are an important part of our national lift'. It is, however, not a belief but a mere practice that is contrary to the spirit and teachings of the Koran, and has no Koranic support. There is therefore no reason to permit halal slaughter here, and we should rise in anger against those who export European animals to suffer oriental cruelties and death. Sweden, Switzerland and New Zealand have banned these rituals and live exports: so should we. Where does New Labour the party of compassion stand?

THE EX-SOLDIER
14 JULY 1998

It is the privilege of old fogeys to claim that National Service did them no harm, even, indeed, that those long-distant compulsory two years in the Army were the best of their lives. Such assertions are now mockingly attributed to boneheaded blimps from public schools who, at 18, were unfit for further education and unfit, after six or seven years of sodomy, fagging, beating, cold showers and breaking the ice in washrooms in winter, for the company of women and any kind of civilised life other than the clubs of St James's and Pall Mall.

Of some young subalterns in smart cavalry regiments this may well have been true, for they inherited the caste and customs of their families and were expected by their senior officers to be the conforming butterflies of the battalion and the mess, with antique epaulettes of chain-mail, red stripes down their narrow trousers and spurs clinking on their heels, but it was a different matter for the East End boy plucked from the comfortable bosom of his mother.

It was the East End boys who found the first weeks in a training battalion hard to bear; they could not darn socks or sew buttons on their uniforms, polish boots, fold blankets or make sense of kit inspections; they lagged behind in the domestic chores of the barrack room, and responded with dismay to the shouts and bullying of non-commissioned officers, men of their own class. Some, after a day spent uncomprehending and wet-through on the battleground and an evening spent burnishing their boots with spoon and spittle, or shaving the coarse whiskers of their trousers so that they would take a better crease and itch less in their crotches, cried themselves to sleep in exhaustion and misery. Yet out of this misery emerged a sense of unity and mutual support, the realisation that a boy was not only responsible for himself, but to some degree for every other boy in the platoon, and that the platoon, and thus the individuals within it, could only function competently if there was, as it were, an exchange of abilities, a helping hand given on the assault course by one, neat skill with the sewing needle by another. From this came loyalty, responsibility, reliance and unselfishness – qualities that survived far into adult life.

Taking boys out of the labour market for two years must have worked marvels for the unemployment figures of the day, and to put them back into it with an adult attitude to life was an even greater marvel. Many returned to civvy street in possession of a skill or trade taught them by the Army, to which they could, perhaps, never have aspired without the benefit of National Service. Boys who knew nothing when they first reported to Aldershot at 18, at 20 were experienced engineers, electricians, drivers of heavy goods vehicles, linguists, typists, accountants and cooks, and were to an employer an entirely different proposition from the loutish, unskilled labourers that they had been before their National Service.

As for the boys to whom none of this applied, who regarded National Service as an intolerable interruption between school and university or school and a profession – they got their comers knocked off and were far the better for it.

What happens now to a young man who leaves the regular Army? Take John, for example, retiring at 26, after 10 years begun as a junior leader and ended as a sergeant in the Royal Artillery, the Gulf War and three tours of Bosnia under his belt – what has he to offer a civilian employer that distinguishes him from 1,000 other applicants for work? He could drop a mortar on 10 Downing Street with pinpoint accuracy, but, whatever we think of Tony Blair, there's not much call for such a skill. He can drive, but so can most boys with unbroken voices and little pubic hair. He can run 10 miles and more over rough country without breaking into a breathless sweat, but what's the use of that? He is sane and sensible, but not educated in any way that an intellectual might recognise, and will struggle dutifully through the memoirs of an army officer, but not a daily broadsheet. He has no cultural interests or experience, and his conversation inevitably reverts to army matters.

John is a creature of the Army, boy and man; to join it was his ambition, to stay with it his obsession, but it is, he says like an old man, no longer what it was when he joined it, and he has had enough. Gone are the days when a non-commissioned officer might remain a soldier into late middle age – gone are the grizzled warrant officers and sergeant-majors who held battalions together and saved their subalterns from arrant folly; the Army is now a younger body and offers no man a lifetime career.

John at only 26 has reached his zenith, and though conditioned mentally and physically to be its devoted and unquestioning instrument, he can see nothing more for himself within the institution that has been his life: he is like a monk who has for a decade recited all the offices from Lauds to Compline, but who must leave his monastery without his faith – and what use are Lauds and Compline in the outside world? What awaits this young man who helped bring peace to Bosnia and as a boy fought in the Gulf War for the rich nabobs of Kuwait? Jobs in uniformed security and supermarkets with wretched pay and unsocial hours are all that are on offer, and if he holds out too long, it may be that we shall see him on the street with *The Big Issue*.

If the Army has changed so much since the days of National Service, it should surely confront this problem and teach its men not only the skills of killing, but the skills of survival back in civvy street – which means a civilian career rather than a dead-end job. John has been taught nothing, and knowing how to boil an egg would serve him better now than all the mortars dropped on Serbs in the environs of Sarajevo.

In all the reorganisation of the armed forces announced last week there was, of course, no mention of this matter, but if the Secretary of State for Defence, the Minister of State for the Armed Forces and those officers who have daily charge of them have any sense of responsibility for the men they employ, they should look to their long-term welfare as much as to their short-term exploitation as fighting men. There is life after the Army, and men should be properly prepared for it.

A CULTURAL DEBT
28 JULY 1998

Sixty years ago, in July 1938, the Dresslers arrived in London, Arthur, Lisbet and Gisela. They came from Hamburg, and the evidence of a once comfortable and cultivated background lay in their few pieces of Biedermeier furniture, two greyish-yellow landscape paintings by a minor Dutchman which were small enough to carry in a raincoat pocket, one splendid Meissen dish, and their books.

Arthur had been a merchant, importing coffee to a great international maritime city where its consumption had become a life-blood ritual. He was, at first sight, German through and through, and could as easily have been a Hanseatic banker portrayed centuries before by Holbein or Durer, as in his own day by Dix or Grosz or Schad. He thought himself a German – and so he should, for he was a graduate of Gottingen University, where the myth of Aryan purity began, and had a duelling scar to show for it, and he had been an officer in the German armies that had devastated France in the Great War – but some interfering Nazi busybody had discovered and disclosed a Jewish grand-mother on his mother's side, and that half pint of Jewish blood the authorities had declared sullying enough to bring about his expulsion from the Nazi Heimat.

That Lisbet was as pure a Pomeranian as could be, her ancestors among the knightly crusaders of the north who had taken

A CULTURAL DEBT

Christianity to the far end of the Baltic, mattered not at all – to those who embraced the Swastika, she was the wife of a Jew and the mother of Gisela, a Jewess.

They were allowed to leave Germany. And, with permission to take with them to the ship as much as could be packed into one small van, it was characteristic of Arthur that he weighed it down with books – the German equivalent of the *Encyclopaedia Britannica* and books on German art, which is where I come into the picture, for in 1941 the Dresslers, on their release from the discomforts of internment, became our neighbours, and air raids and shortages of food brought us together.

My stepfather compared First World War experiences with Arthur, my mother taught Lisbet to cook tripe with milk, and Gisela showed me her father's books – books with coloured reproductions of yellow naked bodies and green faces, of blue horses and toppling rickety architecture, and of mysterious abstract images, neat and finicky by Klee, tempestuous by Kandinsky. After all these years the Dresslers' library still affects me, the few books I have from it as much an Open Sesame now as then, nourishing my knowledge and enthusiasm; that it does so is, in small part, a symbol of the change that occurred in English cultural life as the direct consequence of the expulsion of the Jews from Germany and central Europe in the years immediately before the war broke out in September 1939.

In music these Jews brought with them new standards of performance and interpretation, and those of us who knew only the turbid sounds of the Henry Wood tradition were suddenly aware of unheard subtleties and clarities in the great sweeps of orchestral sound in Beethoven and Wagner, and in the trios and quartets of Schubert and his peers the playing had never been so spirited and spiritual, so perfectly precise and in accord, yet the voice of each instrument so exquisitely distinct.

To the visual arts the Jews brought a broader connoisseurship than was current here. They knew, of course, the respected contemporary artists of Germany, the painters and sculptors whose work had been damned as degenerate in 1937 and burned in 1938, including Oskar Schlemmer, who spoke for all of them with the last words in his diary in 1943 – 'Art is not to be considered as a representation of the world, but its transformation into the wonderful'; these Jews had bought, sold and collected with an informed passion that we have not seen since.

They knew, too, the obscure artists of the past, in Italy and Holland as well as Germany, and they threw themselves and us into the study of old master drawings, those observations, experiments and whims that give such astonishing insights into the artist's mind, with an intensity of response and understanding that far outclassed the average English collector. They broadened the scope of our galleries and museums, and dented our belief that no art of any quality had ever come from beyond the Rhine.

In London University they transformed the study of art history at the Courtauld Institute from the amateur business of the finishing school into a discipline of extreme intellectual austerity, and at the Warburg Institute tied it to the wider history of ideas, so that for a generation or so London was the world's leading centre of such scholarship. Looking back to my student years I am in awe at the names of those teachers whom I took for granted, to whom I owe so much and at whose feet I sometimes sat – Saxl, Gombrich, Ettlinger, Wittkower, Kurz, Demus, Grabar, Pächt, Friedlander and Grete Ring – but I owe most of all to Johannes Wilde, himself not Jewish, but married to Julia, who was. These were they who taught me that to look at a painting is not to read a dated document, but to adventure into the spirit and humanity of man. Who now remembers Johannes, formidably demanding as a teacher yet gentle with those who could not keep the pace? Who can now recall the querulous voice of Kurz, the boom of Pacht, the throaty gutteral of Ettlinger, the trembling lower lip of Lili Fröhlich? Who in London University knows how Aby Warburg's great library of intellectual mysteries came into its maw?

The last war was a filthy business, but without it this country would have remained a cultural backwater much longer, for those who fled here from the Nazi persecutions in the late Thirties immeasurably enriched our lives in art, music, opera, drama, literature, mathematics, science and even broadcasting. Most were Jews, as were those whose lives were extinguished in the gas chambers and whose bodies guttered into greasy smuts up furnace chimneys, but some were homosexuals or Slavs, and some were driven by communist loyalties and Christian consciences; for far the better they changed the lives of all of us, and we owe them an unacknowledged debt.

They deserve some permanent memorial – not a rival to Rodin's Calais Burghers, but a Legenda Aurea, a book of saints. Will no one write it before it is too late, before the last of their very few remaining peers departs for oblivion and all their students cross the Styx in Charon's ferry? Of the Dresslers, apart from a few books and my clear memory, no trace remains.

ANTI-SEMITISM
14 JULY 1998

Anti-Semitism is alive and well in London. Alive and well? How can one use this phrase in this context? Alive and kicking is more suitable, alive and sick the truth. Last month I wrote a column in melancholy praise of the German and other middle European Jewish scholars to whom, and to whose cultural influence, I owe so much, for July marked the 60th anniversary of the arrival in this country of the family that is for me a synecdochism of these many Jews, the small part that stands for the much larger whole. It engendered much correspondence and my brief list of art historians was enhanced by longer lists of Jewish scientists, philosophers, writers and musicians whose determined belief in the relevance to daily life of their intellectual and aesthetic interests has shaped the lives and careers of many Englishmen of my generation.

Many recalled teachers whose ability to inspire their pupils was not to be checked by a shaky hold on a language learned in middle age; many recalled, as I do, their wonderment at what they heard on the BBC's Third Programme when it broke the mould of homely broadcasting – impossible without the Jewish enlightenment that let loose the English intellectual – a pinnacle of achievement from which John Birt and his immediate predecessors have inexorably descended into the banalities of Radio 3.

ANTI-SEMITISM

There were, however, other letters. The first few of the flood I read with disbelief. These, too, took me back into the past, but to events and happenings outside my experience, to the history of the years between the wars, to the British fascists, to the riots in the East End, to the refusal of the British government to acknowledge the persecution of the Jews in Germany, and to the epithet 'Bloody Jew' that tripped so easily from the tongue of every class.

We may no longer hear it now, but it poured from the pens of those who headed their letters with such legends as 'End Jewish Rule in Britain Now', and 'Why did we shut down the gas chambers'? These, too, sent me their lists – of Jews in government (Jack Straw, Home Secretary, is in truth, they tell me, Jacob Stravinsky, a Russian Jewish immigrant), of Jews among the Conservative opposition masquerading with false noses and false names as English gentlemen, of the Jews who dominate the medical professions, banking, business and the law and other entertainments. None quite reached the point of telling me that Archbishop Carey is a Jew, but some ordinary bishops in the Church of England were identified as circumcised.

No political, professional or financial aspect of our lives is free of a pervasive Jewish influence to their advantage and gentile impoverishment, it seems, and along with the homosexual mafia we have a Jewish mafia to fear. 'We want treason trials,' ranted one extremist, 'It's time for the Jews to move on again,' argued another, and repatriation was the demand most often made.

Repatriation where? Jew is a word that embraces many centuries of harsh mythology. Christians were long taught – indeed until well into this century – that the Jews were responsible for Christ's crucifixion, howling for his blood. Armenians, the oldest of Christian peoples, brought to the west, even to St Alban's in 1228, the tale of the Jew who taunted

Jesus with 'Get a move on, you're holding up the traffic' as he passed his door carrying the cross, to receive Christ's only curse, 'I go, but thou shalt wait till I return, wandering restless over the whole earth.'

Thus Ahasuerus became the Wandering Jew, the cobbler in Dusseldorf, the diamond cutter in Amsterdam, the tortured victim of the Inquisition in Madrid; he, too, stands as a synecdochism – for the diaspora that began with the expulsion from Eden and continues still, that spread from ancient Egypt into the antique world of Greece, Rome and farthest Persia, that colonised Byzantium and Spain, and built Synagogues from the Rhine to deep Siberia. In all these they set themselves apart, the Chosen People, in their obstinate observance of circumcision, the Sabbath and their dietary laws, inspiring primitive mistrust and the fear that is its twin. 'How odd of God to choose the Jews.'

Like the Jew himself, the word Jew carries the baggage of at least 3,000 years of cultural antipathy, and a man must be careful how he says it; said with sympathy it lays him open to extreme abuse from the anti-Semitic, said without, he is exposed to unwelcome charges of racial prejudice. Dago, Wop, Frog, Hun, Kraut – all these familiars now have a good-humoured element in their use and are no more wholly abusive and contemptuous than Scouse and Mick and Jock; one might reasonably argue that their implied disrespect can be a perverse but jocular expression of affection, and for using them one would certainly not expect to be hauled before the Race Relations Board. Yid, however, their equivalent, one must never use at all, and even with Jew one must be wary with the tone and timbre of voice, for what should be an identification of origin as uncluttered as Scot or German can be both uttered and heard as an accusation, as a word of utmost scorn.

ANTI-SEMITISM

The writers of my unwanted letters were too cowardly to sign them. I had to make what I could of Croydon and a squiggle. They gave me no formal 'Dear Mr...' but began with the words 'Jew Lover' and 'You must be a Jew yourself' embellished with bloody and the F-word. I learned to recognise the envelopes, for most of these correspondents could not resist the compulsion to continue with a slogan or admonition for the postman's benefit or an insult of some kind; many stuck their stamps upside down, and I suppose this to be a talisman of some kind, a curse or voodoo practice.

I felt sullied by these letters; I read them all, dutifully, the analytical part of my brain noting their poor command of grammar, the syntactical disorder, the underlying hysteria that banished reason, and some might say that I should have pitched them at once into the waste-bin. Yet I sought enlightenment, a reason and a reasoned argument, a sound intellectual statement in support of a view that I do not and cannot share. But there was nothing to respect in any of them; instead, they left me only with the need to wash, to clean my hands of the touch of paper touched by these writers; and I felt, too, the need that I last felt when the Saatchi collection of Britpack art was exhibited at the Royal Academy – the need to walk home through trees and grass and things pure and natural, purging my mind of their obscenities. How can any Englishman harbour such vile medieval prejudice?

POISSON EN GELÉE
8 SEPTEMBER 1998

Fish heads, underpants and lilies – an unlikely salmagundi of a subject for anything other than a surrealist painting or an extra verse to Tweedledee's song of shoes and ships and sealing wax, cabbages and kings. Improbable fellows they may be, but they have a kinship of sorts in my local supermarkets. Let us take the fish heads first. '*Poisson en gelée*,' mused Mary in the early morning sun, 'now that would be good to eat in this hot weather.' Of uncertain age, but post-Edwardian by a decade or two, educated when French was the whole world's diplomatic language and all things Parisian were deemed the epitome of style, refinement and good taste, her knowledge of them garnished with romantic experience of the Levant when, from Istanbul to Alexandria, it was still exotic, intellectual and raffish, Mary's musings deserve a better audience than her fellow dog-walkers in the dew of Kensington Gardens.

'And how is that made?' I enquired. 'Oh any fish will do as long as it can be flaked or forced into a pulp through a strainer; add peeled pink shrimps for colour and a handful of *petite pois* for contrast, set in aspic. We begin with fish heads, boiled to make the jelly, and with fins and tails if we can find them. I shall go straightway to Sainsbury's and see.'

And so she did. The estimable brothers Sainsbury do indeed sell fish heads – at 40 pence a pound. Mary waited while the

94

woman ahead of her bought a whole salmon. 'Do you want the head?' asked the red-fisted boy behind the counter. 'Ugh no!' the disgusted response. 'But I do,' interjected Mary. 'Then give it to this lady,' said the woman. 'Can't do that,' said the boy. 'Why not?' the woman's response. 'Well, only of she pays for it.' 'But it's my fish head, and I have paid for it. Put it in a separate bag and I will give it to her.' 'Can't do that,' repeated the boy, 'unless, of course, you promise not to give it to her until you've both left the premises. You can give it to her outside, but not in.'

At this point Mary cried 'Stop, stop, *n'importe quoi*! Enough of this job's-worth rigmarole. I will pay for the head of the salmon.' In the telling of the tale her smoker's voice had sunk a register or two and her 'I will pay for the head of the salmon' adopted the sinister growling timbre of that marvellous line in Richard Strauss's Salome, 'Bring me the head of John the Baptist'.

Forty pence a pound seems quite a whack to charge for fish heads – and pure profit to boot on the 'where there's muck, there's brass' principle. Of course, the saintly brothers (to sain is to bless or to save from evil influence) will argue that they have to pay the boy with raw hands and provide space on the slab, that the plastic bag, the time involved, and the certainty that every dotty old bat taken by the sudden whim to make *poisson en gelée* will always find the fish heads with which to make the sticky stock, must all have a cost to be recovered with a profit.

It is, of course, an acceptable argument until we realise that customers have already paid for the fish heads at the full price per pound of salmon, halibut and dory, and then made a gift of them to the vendor. To add another 40 pence to the £9.45 or £5.99 per pound already paid for turbot and bass, money already tucked away in the till, is to derive from the sale of these inedible parts the extortionate profit of the usurer. Surely the fishmonger should enquire if his customer wants the head before he weighs and prices the fish, not after, for only if the head is refused and not paid for is he then perfectly entitled to charge another customer his extra 40 pence for it.

The old adage 'Twice given stinks,' applied to re-used wedding presents, adapted to 'Twice sold,' is fitting here.

While Mary was doing battle for her fish heads, I was in British Home Stores buying bargain underpants. I dare say that I am perceived as a man either of silken sensibilities in that quarter, or given to the natty little things that we import from Messrs Horn and Klein, but neither of these is so – dowdy grey cotton is my choice, cheap and far from cheerful, easy to discard without a qualm when the fabric wearies and the elastic sags. They come in packs of three for £10, but the shelf bore the seductive legend 30 per cent off. I queued with three packs instead of one and £21 in my hand. The boy at the counter demanded £30. 'No, no. They are reduced,' I said. 'Not according to this,' said the boy, pointing to the till. We were at an impasse: the till was adamant at £30 and so was I at £21. He rang a bell; we waited; the queue behind me grew turbulent at the delay and 'You'd think he could afford thirty quid without making a fuss,' said a voice from somewhere in its snaking length. A sulky girl decked in authority eventually appeared; the boy explained; she fiddled with the till, keyed a new instruction into it, and went her way without gentling smile or murmur of apology. Coming away with my bargain offer, I wondered how many men had paid the full price for underpants without noticing that they'd been rooked.

From Bhs I went to Marks & Spencer to buy lilies and practice mental arithmetic, a discipline in which I have since infancy been useless. I dislike the lily, its perfume is sickly sweet and it appeared in far too many of the pious pictures to which I was exposed in my Catholic childhood, the attribute of such obscure saints with Lawks a' Mercy upturned eyes as Euphemia, a virgin of late and unreliable legend, and Scholastica, patroness of Benedictine nunneries, as well as of the Archangel Gabriel in effete, androgynous, even hermaphrodite guise as the messenger of the Annunciation. I buy them only because my bossy women friends tell me that when they come I must camouflage the bachelor bleakness of my house with as many flowers as I can afford. Lilies last a fortnight if properly nurtured, and though initially expensive, represent the best value.

Marks & Sparks sell them ready wrapped at £4.99 for five stems, and I buy three bunches at a time. Recently they have had bigger bunches marked '£14.99 for 20 per cent more.' With the sane man's interest in more for less I hauled one out of the tub, only to find it light in weight and small in bulk. I turned it upside down and counted the stalks to find that there were 12.

Now I am in no intellectual condition to argue this point with obstinacy, but it seemed to me that M&S were offering the contrary blandishment of less for more, and that numbskulls of my ilk were likely to be confused into paying £14.99 for 12 stems in one bunch instead of £14.97 for 15 in three. The '20 per cent more' clearly applies to the price rather than the number of blooms.

Now M&S were nice enough when I complained that their bananas were bruised and mushy within unblemished skins, and sent me away burdened with fresh fruit, and Sainsbury's could not have been more attentive and subservient when I found household moths fluttering busily in a sealed bag of their muesli, but I suspect that both, and I suspect BHS too – though I have had no other cause to murmur against them, and their underpants have proved commendably robust – all err in their own favour when adjusting prices and issuing instructions to their tills, or fail to consider every factor when putting a price on the discarded heads of fish.

These errors are, no doubt, occasional rather than habitual, and in the great electronic hurly-burly of the supermarket world must be forgiven, but, unlike Mary's *poisson en gelée*, eaten with a salad of chopped garlic, parsley, olives and white beans, they leave a nasty taste – of suspicion and lost trust.

PAEDOPHILIA
22 SEPTEMBER 1998

Paedophilia fatigue is upon us. Scotland Yard identified yet another paedophile ring last week with all the usual ramifications of long-term abuse masked by professional respectability and good charitable works with links all over Europe and the sorry business of missing children, their faces staring mindless out of thousands of photographs recording their grim sexual experience in the hands of adults. News of it reached radio, television and the papers, but editors grow weary of repeated sin and the reports were cursory – the mixture as before, whether in the wilds of Wales or the stews of London, does not make good headlines, and world weariness stills the reader's shudder.

For an adult to engage in sexual activity with an adolescent may, in our society's eyes, be wrong, both legally and socially, but it is not unnatural – you have only to cross the borders of western Europe to find the child bride perfectly acceptable, pupping babies in her very early teens. Here in England, however, we go into a Lawks a' Mercy condition of dismay whenever an adult woman hauls a boy into her bed for lessons in lubricity, and men who do the same with girls, even if separated by only two or three years, we send to jail. 'And you don't have to be queer to enjoy a bit of buggery with boys,' said a married man in my local pub, with a twinkle in his eye and two demure daughters back at home – one of the more honest responses to my soundings on paedophilia.

Where do we draw the line, for draw it we must. Lowering the age of consent to 16 is a perfectly reasonable compromise, though most boys know much earlier their sexual destiny – heterosexual or homosexual – and the law should have considerable discretion in both fields to ignore this defining line in many circumstances. Can we safely drop below 16? For most adolescents we probably could (and perhaps should), but an age of consent at 15 might put a measurable number of immature adolescents in moral and physical jeopardy – a number that would greatly increase if the age of consent were lowered to 14, 13 or 12, though most children are, at this lowest figure, in some sense sexually active. An age of consent at 14 might have saved the life of Jason Swift, a rent boy murdered to keep his silence about his abduction and rape.

But even at 12 we have not reached the age at which many paedophiles come into play; some, of course, are satisfied with children on the verge of puberty, but others want them much younger, and it is at this vague point that our horror is justified – a horror that grows stronger the nearer we come to the infant and the babe in arms, for with these, sexual abuse is no longer an assault on the supposed innocence that we cherish in our children, but is a physical abuse quite appalling in its implications. Sex with small children is either an abuse of power or a symptom of intellectual paedomorphism, by which I mean that in the adult brain some arrest has occurred that keeps the physically developed adult at an infantile stage of sexuality. Neither should be tolerated, or excused.

Most of us are trained not to be sexually opportunist with minors, nor to give sexual expression to our power over them, but some adults fall into temptation when minors are knowingly provocative – an aspect of the problem rarely acknowledged by authority, yet a common cause of consensual activity that hardly counts as abuse.

Some offenders, caught and shamed, will never offend again and are harmless, but others are habitual and present the problem that we must not fail to solve – the problem, at its most extreme, of the child-killer driven by utterly selfish lust. How is it, we should ask ourselves, that Sidney Cooke, the man who killed Jason Swift, is more or less free to roam our streets?

We talk of justice and the penalty paid. We should talk of the 14-year-old boy whom society in some sense had condemned to prostitution – voice just breaking, his skinny body almost hairless, his upper lip scarcely ever in need of the razor's drag, buggered to death – to put no fine point on it. And this was manslaughter, the penalty served a mere nine years in jail for Sidney Cooke, whose name echoes yet again in this latest case.

Did justice decide that the life of a boy prostitute was virtually worthless? That he brought his death upon himself? That he would never have grown into a worthy citizen? That we don't really need to worry about homosexuals? Good riddance perhaps? Maybe.

In this latest paedophile ring some of the victims, mostly boys, have been as young as eight. I know it is foul, but think of it - a boy of eight with an adult penis in his mouth or thrusting at his anal sphincter, a girl of eight, her hymen broken. Is a year or two in jail sufficient penalty for this? Should any other child be put at risk of another such misdemeanour in the name of justice for the offender?

I know that my research is merely anecdotal and burdened with prejudice, but I will risk asserting that paedophiles are plausible dissemblers, scheming and deceitful, single-minded in the management of their lives so that their contact with children has a seeming legitimacy, and utterly without scruple.

These men are not homosexual in any sense that applies to most men of that fraternity, who are largely indifferent to boys, or sentimental about them and harmless. Boys have nothing to fear from them. These men are not even paedophiles, for if the roots of this fashionable word mean anything, it is that they are child lovers – but the lust that they feel for children has nothing of love and tenderness in it, and no lover of boys would have sent Jason Swift to his death, nor Sidney Cooke's earlier victims, Mark Tildesley, aged seven, and Barry Lewis, aged six.

My impression is that the conventions of justice should not apply in these cases, and that men convicted of serious child abuse should be abandoned by society. The ages of those so far identified in this latest case reveal that the inclination to have sex with children does not abate – 49, 50, 60, 66 and 78. Should we imprison them for life – by which we must mean until their dying day? Should we establish an island colony for them in the Outermost Hebrides and let them fend for themselves or starve? Should we pay the French to send them to Devil's Island?

We cannot hang or mutilate them but we must do something beyond the bounds of present punishment that effectively excludes them forever from our society.

CHINA AND
THE COLA CAN
29 SEPTEMBER 1998

The most offensive detail of the Clinton Affair was not that the President of the United States, the most powerful man in the world (cue: trumpet blasts and a chorus of 'Hail to the Chief'), performed oral sex with the nubile and all-too-willing Monica. Compared with Ivan the Terrible and Catherine the Great, the Emperor Tiberius and Lloyd George (surely that song should have been 'Lloyd George knew my Mother'?), and all the lecherous Borgias, this act of sexual prowess was modest in the extreme (kid stuff, indeed) – so modest that Clinton could not reconcile it with any definition of sexual congress of which he was aware. And how could that be, an English audience might ask, assuming one act of sexual penetration to be much the same as another? To that the answer lies in a cultural distinction that, like the Atlantic, divides the English-speaking people.

On one of the evenings that in the mid-Sixties I spent in Andy Warhol's New York Factory (Et in Arcadia, Ego), early enough for the languid and beautiful young things still to be conscious, they debated at some length the business of oral sex. To an Englishman this was then a disconcerting preliminary, an element of foreplay, if it took place at all, but to Americans it was, and still is, a satisfactory end in itself.

The Warhol debate was over the nature of the roles adopted by the participants, which active and which passive. The shrewd mind of a Jesuit would have been valuable in bringing discipline to the discussion, which in the smog of cannabis became ever more confused and self-revelatory, but the general conclusion, surprising to an Englishman who tends to see oral penetration as an aggressive act, was that the recipient is the active partner, the driving force – a conclusion confirmed by an extraordinary American film, *Deep Throat*, in which a young woman with clitoral tonsils performed amazing feats of sword-swallowing so to speak – a plot well worth reviving with Miss Lewinsky in the title role.

If the attitude of Americans to oral sex is formed by heavy petting sessions in the backs of Chevrolets when they are adolescents – there the boys lie, thinking of England (as it were) while the girls get on with it – then I can understand Clinton's evasions in his taped evidence to the grand jury, for the inquisition must have seemed to him culturally incomprehensible, the words 'Oh come on, fellows, we've all done it, you know what it's like as well as I do,' constantly springing to his lips.

The American nation seems to have recognised this, even if the grand jury and the leaders of the Republican Party have not, and one wrinkled old potato-grower in Idaho summoned before the vox pop TV camera, said it for them all with his 'There are only three people concerned in this affair: two enjoyed themselves and one don't care.' But would that have been his dismissal of the hoo-ha had Miss Lewinsky been Miss Whip in fetish leather, or worse, been a boy?

If Clinton survives this crisis it will be because the ordinary men and women of America, far more honest than lawyers and politicians, recognise that his extramarital pleasures were satisfying the appetites of an active, healthy, full-blooded man, and heave a sigh of relief that they were so straightforward and in some degree the common experience of them all. We, in Europe, having no political axe to grind, should share this generous view and retrain both from baying for his resignation and sniggering at his exposure. We and he should return to the business of keeping the world on an even keel. I am grateful that he has willy-nilly brought a new frankness into conversation and that never again shall the chattering classes feel the need to blush and fumble for a euphemism – oh how I envy the company of those who customarily call a f*** a f***.

One thing, however, I shall neither forgive Clinton, nor forget – the sight of his swigging cola from a can while confronting the grand jury. If he deserves impeachment for anything it is not the what, where, when and how of the ample Monica, but swigging from a can. Are there no glasses in the White House? Are his servants so offended by the carpet stains that they have abandoned him? Are his aides so negligent that they cannot attend to a minor matter of decorum? Have all the highest levels of American society fallen so low that they no longer have china, glass and cutlery? Have the ancient and genteel families recorded in the Social Register, that *Almanach de Gotha* of American aristocracy, taken to the gutter?

To drink from a can is unseemly, but the beastly habit is now common here; so too is drinking from the bottle, but this is now the expectation of some pub landlords who express surprise when anyone asks for a glass, their laddish response suggesting that one must, to be so effete, be a pansy. The young now seem to be in constant need of fluids, travelling everywhere with can and bottle in hand, littering the streets with their discards. They have long been in constant need of food, ditching the unwanted remains of chicken and chips in gutters and front gardens and adding to the hazards of the Underground. In the offices of this newspaper, adolescent writers who are well able to escape for lunch consume beef bourguignon and baked beans at their desks and the wastepaper bins are a-slop with the remains. We have adopted these customs from America where food on the trot is part of their culture of immediate satisfaction – a twinge of hunger, and down goes a Dunkin' Donut laden with fat and sugar, the slightest hint of thirst, and into a drugstore they go to slake it with a can of cola. And now, it seems, so do we; the street has become our dining-room, the dumping-ground for its discarded rubbish, and our vomitorium.

Bill Clinton is not, of course, to blame for the sloppy business of eating in the street, though he may well be responsible for a worldwide increase in the practice of fellatio, but he set a poor example with his can of cola, and that he could do so indicates that his own standard of behaviour has been allowed to slip. The small civilising ceremonies of food and drink lie at the heart of family life and social interaction and are essential courtesies – we abandon them at our peril.

It may seem an absurd and trifling matter, but the publicly swigging Clinton with a can in his hand was for me much more a symbol of the breakdown of society than the private Clinton with pouting Monica before him on her embroidered and emblazoned tailored knee-pads.

MULTIPLE SCLEROSIS
3 NOVEMBER 1998

Readers will forgive me if, in my dotage, I remember October 1998 not for the Ron Davies affair, nor for the Jenkins proposals for a reform of the way we vote, and certainly not for the mischievous and ill-written tittle-tattle of Penny Junor's researches into the disintegration of the Charles and Diana marriage, but for an entirely personal matter that I cannot discharge from my mind. Four years ago, in October 1994, I had a heart attack. I had no idea what was happening to me; the initial pains could have been entirely muscular, the nausea could have been caused by something eaten the night before, the sweats could have been the sudden onset of influenza, and the pins and needles in my hands and feet... but the combination of these phenomena was beyond the ready explanation that I sought. By the time the ambulance came, pain had destroyed my ability to think, and I could neither move nor speak.

It was the beginning of a long and tedious business – of semi-surgical interventions, drugs that numbed the brain, unappetising restrictions in diet, a quadruple by-pass and a pacemaker that scrapes against my bones every time I move. I puff and blow with every exertion, cannot climb stairs, cannot run after buses, cannot play tennis, cannot ski, cannot blunder about in mountains, cannot, cannot, cannot... I am angry, resentful and, I suppose, self-pitying – that is, I was, until halfway through October when a cheeky young man in a wheelchair challenged me in the National Gallery. It is a rare thing to sense, immediately, equality and balance in a casual encounter, and too good a thing to carelessly let go. He came to lunch a few days later at my friendly local restaurant, and it was in transferring him from the wheelchair to the table that I began to see the extent of his disability. In the same month that I had my first heart attack, multiple sclerosis struck him: he was 24, tall, well-built, conventionally handsome – even now the rugby forward is still discernible. But four years on, at 28, the frame is gaunt, the clothes hang loose, and the hands are feeble – 'I can't manage a knife very well,' he said with matter-of-fact charm, 'could you cut it small for me?'

He spoke of MS without anger, without resentment – except for the weekly magazine that had dismissed him with specious excuses as soon as he disclosed the diagnosis – and without self-pity. He spoke of it only because I probed, otherwise his conversation was entirely of art, travel and the pursuits of the civilised mind. I wondered about sex, recalling the dangerous urgency of its demands when I was 28, and kept silent. But I wonder still. And then he announced, as might any man among friends, that he must go to the loo before setting off for home.

The loos in this restaurant are downstairs. Using the backs of chairs for support, and hanging on to me when none was near, he lurched a slow and irregular course through the room and then rested a minute or two against the wall at the top of the stairs. 'I'll go down on my bottom; will you go first and lift my feet onto a lower step?'

And that is how we did it. It seemed quite easy, even a little amusing – and I once got an injured man down a mountain that way – but hauling him to his feet at the bottom and getting him unbruised through the narrow doors to the loo was no easy feat.

MULTIPLE SCLEROSIS

And there was nothing funny about getting him up the stairs, not even Charlie Chaplin could have found humour in that Sisyphusian struggle.

John stood at the bottom holding the handrail, with me behind him. 'Lift my left foot onto the step, and then my right when I've shifted my weight.' And that is what I did. No one who has not lifted a human leg in such a way has any idea of how heavy it can be, or how wayward. I was aware of great bones within the trouser legs, of feet that veered to left or right and could never be placed with accuracy on the narrow treads, of panting with the effort of lifting in a crouch, of sweating indeed, and of my pacemaker behaving like a turbo-boost. A few steps up, first one leg and then the other went into muscle spasm and became uncontrollable. John hauled, I pushed and lifted, and eventually, both of us exhausted, we reached the top. We had taken half an hour.

I do not know what the future holds for him. The cold part of my mind supposes terrible things; the warm part does not want to face them. I could shrug off the business of the stairs, but for John it is part of daily life and getting worse. In the past four years, surgeons and cardiologists have saved my life and left me with something that, though restricted, still has much of the quality to which I am accustomed, but for him there have been no such ingenious interventions, and in the same four years he has had to come to terms with a condition worsening so rapidly that…that what? And why? I understand that MS cannot be cured, but that in the USA some drugs have been identified as encouraging remission in some cases. These drugs are not available in this country: they are too expensive for the NHS, and no patient whose parents and friends, knowing how much damage has already been done and how little time may be left, might club together and fund him for a year or two is permitted to import these drugs for private administration. John would willingly be a guinea pig for them, but this too is not permitted.

If I were he, I would rage against such a prohibition, but he only observes that the NHS has more important matters to attend to – Viagra, for example.

I can think of no tragic work of art that has touched me more. Compared with John's predicament, the downfall of Ron Davies is a comedy and the Jenkins report material for a farce. Neither is worth a second thought, but the fate of young John is: think how much the meagre quality of his life will be diminished when the failing fingers can no longer control the wheelchair, when he can no longer undo the buttons of his trousers or lift a glass of water to his lips. Should he not be allowed to try, at the expense of those who love him, a might-or-might-not drug?

I have for some time campaigned for the spread of clear, uncluttered information about the heart, for no one who has not had an attack can imagine in even the slightest degree the exquisite agony involved, and Torquemada devised no torment more refined – but MS seems to me an insidious thing far more terrible.

CIRCUMCISION
7 DECEMBER 1999

Throughout this year circumcision has simmered on the back burner, the lid of the casserole occasionally lifted by the World Health Organisation, a Commons Select Committee, the children's charity Unicef, Clare Short's Department of International Development and, as the official debate has been entirely on the matter of female circumcision, by Miss Germaine Greer. To everyone's surprise, this venerated sibyl of Saffron Walden is in favour of it, and just as Lewis Carroll's Queen of Hearts was given to shouting 'Off with her head' without a moment's thought, so dear Germaine is inclined to bellow 'Off with her labia. Out with her clitoris', arguing that these excisions are a cultural right with which we in the irreligious West have no business to interfere.

Had we, I wonder, any business to interfere with cannibalism in the Congo? Should we have tolerated the roasting of young missionaries and the boiling of old as a natural hazard of the job, rather than upset the equanimity of some barbaric Mrs Beeton?

Barbaric? A dangerous word to use in the context of some 30 African and Middle Eastern cultures in these prickly days of political correctitude, but barbaric female circumcision is, and with livid scarring, not a pretty sight. Absurd though both male and female organs must seem to the airy-fairy aesthete, in the ordinary western mortal they stimulate all the necessary responses in their natural state, and in their natural state they should be left, whether female or male, except in cases of phimosis.

Barbaric? Anecdotal evidence has it that thousands of female circumcisions take place in Britain every year, but unlike France and Italy, no one has ever been prosecuted for performing them, though the children of immigrant communities may well have British citizenship. Think of it – that pretty little dark-skinned creature who is your daughter's schoolfriend may, at any moment, be held down by the women in her family and mutilated by one of them with nothing more surgical than a razor and hot water.

I have not seen it – no man can, for it is women's business – but I have witnessed the circumcision of a Muslim boy and would not wish such an experience on my worst enemy. Ahmed was six and well developed for his age. In the crowded room, decorated with phallic balloons, the puzzled child in pyjama trousers was passed to his father, seated on an upright chair, and stood quietly when the cord was untied. The man with the knife swabbed behind the foreskin and then pulled it forward over the tumescence. Ahmed snivelled, his father wiped his nose, settled him for a moment on his knees and then looped his forearms under and between the boys thighs, and gripped his wrists. Ahmed was thus pinioned, bottom hanging low, knees wide apart, crutch thrust forward and hands well out of the way. A fresh blade was unwrapped and fitted to the razor, and with the foreskin pulled painfully forward by an instrument resembling pliers, the deed was done. An astonishing quantity of blood spurted from the wound, most of it onto my trousers, some of it, and the foreskin, into the plastic bowl below. Ahmed screamed and men called his name and snapped their fingers to distract him, but he screamed and screamed. Then the stitching

CIRCUMCISION

began, a cat's cradle of a business with the tiny bloody penis tugged here and there as the stitches tightened and the profuse bleeding was reduced to a welling ooze. We watched in silence as the last drops of blood slowly gathered on the glans and fell away. The tiny penis, straight before this brutal surgery began, now veered to the left; the foreskin was tipped into the lavatory, and Ahmed into bed, whimpering with pain and fright. A female circumcision, so much larger in extent, so much longer in duration, so much more radical in that it involves the removal of the instrument of pleasure, must subject its victim to extreme surgical shock.

The significance of the rite of circumcision is much disputed – it began as a tribal rite of initiation or recognition of fitness for marriage, to promote fertility, or as a synecdochism for human sacrifice; we suppose much, but know no answers. In the Christian West we know it as a Jewish rite as old as Genesis dating from Abraham's self-inflicted circumcision at the age of 99 as confirmation of his covenant with God. The practice fell into desuetude while the Israelites were in the wilderness, and when God instructed Joshua to reintroduce it, the Children of Israel must have felt great relief when the backlog had been dispatched and they were able to revert to a rite for infants. The Koran does not specify it, but as Mahomet was circumcised in accordance with Arab custom long before he assumed the mantle of Prophet, no uncircumcised man may make the pilgrimage to Mecca; with the spread of Islam, circumcision rings the globe.

It may be as old as the hunter-gatherers, as old as rings through noses and nipples; Herodotus thought the Egyptians were the first to do it, and there is mummified evidence for his assertion, but he knew nothing of the Aztecs and Amazonian Indians, nor of the Australian Aborigines who so mutilated themselves that they could not ejaculate and must squat like women to empty their bladders. Where circumcision was, and is, the custom, there is very little to be done about it – except here.

There is no reason in support of circumcision – sand under the foreskin in the desert, smegma in the once unwashed North, aesthetic preference (though in classical art the foreskin has always been the first line in decorum, a grace note, so to speak), some primitive belief in the unchastity of women with a clitoris: the human race has always been able to justify stale custom with 'because'. Here we should put an end to it. Poor Ahmed, the perfect child, grew into a man with his penis pointing to the left, but had he been a girl of Somali origin the mutilation would have been the equivalent of castration. Miss Greer is wrong.

EID-EL-KEBIR
7 MARCH 2000

On the 16th day of this month, the Muslim festival of Eid-el-Kebir begins. In Britain, this feast of animal sacrifices passes unnoticed by those who are not Muslims, largely because it is observed by proxy, with money sent to poorer countries where the carcasses are given to the indigent. Its roots lie in the Book of Genesis, in God's so-called Temptation of Abraham when, at the very last moment, his son Isaac, bound hand and foot and lying on what was intended to be his sacrificial altar, was rescued by God's command: 'Lay not thine hand upon the lad.' At that very moment Abraham spied a ram caught in a thicket by its horns and slaughtered it instead.

The symbolism and the abject piety are obvious and the tale is deeply touching – the aged Abraham well past his 100 years, his wife Sarah even older (her death at 127 opens the next chapter), dried up old things for whom Isaac's belated birth had been miraculous. The three of them prefigure the birth and death of Christ and provide rich pickings for Christian theologians who, beginning with St Paul, argued against animal sacrifice (Christ himself preached that sacrifice is subordinate to mercy) and circumcision.

Some 1,700 years after the event, early Christians relinquished animal sacrifice, but in AD 610 or so Islam, founded by Mohammed as the consequence of divine revelation, absorbed

Jewish elements of observance and consolidated animal sacrifice in the new religion. Jewry has since abandoned it, but Islam has not, and it survives in particularly brutal forms among poorly educated Muslims ignorant of the kindly requirements of the Koran, as an essentially superstitious ritual.

Mohammed's Koran teaches that the knife must be razor sharp, but not sharpened in the animal's presence, that the beast must be treated gently and go calmly to its death watered and fed, that no animal should see another slaughtered and that no unnecessary suffering of any kind should be inflicted. A single sweep of the knife should sever the carotid artery, the jugular vein and the windpipe.

All over the Near East, North Africa and elsewhere in the extensive Islamic world, the behests of the Koran will be ignored at this year's Eid-el-Kebir, and there is little we can do about it, just as we have no influence on the daily beastliness of halal slaughter in the happy holiday resorts of Tunisia and Turkey, but the feast is celebrated by Muslim immigrants in Europe, too.

In Britain, when it seemed that what has happened in fields on the outskirts of Paris was about to be repeated in the Essex environs of London, New Labour introduced a Statutory Instrument prohibiting 'slaughter by a religious method elsewhere than in a slaughterhouse', to come into force last March. And what did happen in Paris? A killing field, no less, of which the RSPCA, Compassion in World Farming and responsible newspapers have told us every year since 1996.

The horrors there have stayed much the same in type and number since – sheep in their hundreds, not fed, not watered, their four hooves tightly tied together, thrown on their backs to have their throats cut by the families that have just bought them, the cuts often not immediately lethal, the gurgling,

choking, painful deaths prolonged in the sight of other animals
– with no question of following the dictates of the Koran, no
question of welfare for the animals involved.

And what is our particular interest in this? Most of the sheep
are of British origin, knowingly exported by our caring farmers
to a death, the manner of which is illegal here. It is also illegal
in Europe, but the French authorities, victims (as it were) of
their African empire (just as we are of ours), urge the Brussels
bureaucrats to make allowances for 'sensitive religious, cultural
and ethnic considerations'.

In France an estimated 5,000 sheep were slaughtered by
amateurs, even small boys, last year; this year, the figure is
expected to rise to 8,000. Is it not time for Brussels to compel
the French to put an end to the foul practice? Is it not time
for Muslim immigrants to make allowances for the 'sensitive
religious, cultural and ethnic considerations' of the western
Europeans with whom they wish to live, and abandon offensive
practices in mutual respect? Are we not ethnic too?

Muslims may view these remarks with astonishment and
incomprehension, even resentment, pointing to our own
treatment of farm animals as curious examples of compassion.
We close our local abattoirs so that animals must travel
in overloaded trucks for long hours and many miles to be
slaughtered, distressed by the hazards of the journey, by thirst,
hunger and broken limbs.

The traffic in live animal exports grows again, month on
month, without thought of rough weather on the sea or the
length of journeys to abattoirs in Greece and southern Italy.
What is the Muslim to make of the cruelty with which we breed
bent bones in the battery hen? Check for yourself next time you
eat a thigh or drumstick and see if it is straight. Every year, we
deliver more than one million birds to slaughterhouses already

dead, so cruel are their travelling conditions. We slaughter 9,000 birds an hour and reject nine million corpses as unfit to eat. Of the ducks we cook, 90 per cent have never seen a pond, have never dabbled in water and may well have been blind because of the deprivation. We breed cows to carry ever larger udders, and shoot the calves that bring their mothers into milk.

The Muslim in Paris may well point to foie gras and the poor goose so cruelly crammed with maize that its liver approaches 10 times its normal size and becomes a delicacy for gourmands. The Muslim in London may be very puzzled that we make so much fuss over halal slaughter when we eat so much halal meat curried in his restaurants. The Muslim may wonder at our treatment of wild ponies, heartlessly sold from our moors to the French and Belgian meat markets, and he may well ask how it is that we turn a blind eye to the trade in horses and donkeys from Poland and Lithuania, destined for Italian sausage factories, with more than 100,000 of them trucked every year to abattoirs in the heel of Italy and, worse, across the sea to Sardinia.

With journeys of 1,500 miles or so, and lasting four days or more without food and water, they meet their slaughterers exhausted, dehydrated, trampled, broken-boned, collapsing and often already dead. The same is true of sad little donkey foals imported from Romania for the delicate pink meat of mortadella. Shall we ask the Muslim what he thinks of our hypocrisy when we breed (intelligent) animals for the specific purpose of vivisection, when we import monkeys from the wild, transport them in yet more appalling conditions, and then keep them alive for one dread experiment after another, many of them frivolous, repetitive, mutilating, non-medical and, some might argue, non-scientific? In such circumstances cruelty breeds wanton cruelty.

EID-EL-KEBIR

We are right to be horrified by what happens in France at Eid-el-Kebir, right to demand action from our Ministers of Agriculture and the bureaucrats of Europe, right to seek to put an end to it. Mote and beam, however, mote and beam – if any recall Christ's Sermon on the Mount. We have ourselves much too much to remedy.

BEGGARS
27 MARCH 2000

You are in Istanbul, on holiday. You have spent the day in the
Blue Mosque and Hagia Sophia, or cruising the Bosphorus,
admiring the old Ottoman summer houses and lunching on
fresh fish at a fashionable restaurant. In the great bazaar you have
bought what passes for an antique rug and enough cardamom
and coriander to satisfy the whole of Islington; and now, in the
cool of the evening, refreshed by a shower and clean clothes, you
go for a walk before seeking supper fit for a Levantine prince.

And what do you find? You find that a multitude of beggars have taken their stations on the streets, some very old and
bent, often in pathetic couples, rheumy-eyed, some blind, some
lame and even limbless, shuffling on buttocks, knees and hands
crudely patched in leather, mothers with sleeping children
draped across their folded legs, and wide-eyed prepubescent ur-
chins scrawny with starvation – all with a cupped hand waiting
for a coin, all mute.

Such poverty has long been evident in the old heart of Europe, Russia and the Balkans, where we could ignore it, pass by
on the other side. Now that it is to be seen daily on the streets
of London, we deplore it, not, alas, in the spirit of charity, but
with unseemly spite, spleen, malevolence and anger.

Nightly, it seems, we see or hear those gross harridans Ann
Widdecombe and Barbara Roche compete in gall. 'Unsex me

here,' they cry, 'and fill me full of direct cruelty, stop up the passages of compunction and remorse and pluck my nipple from
the baby's boneless gums' – Lady Macbeth said it at much greater length, but they match her in venom and malign intensity.

To Mrs Roche, the Immigration Minister, begging is 'vile'
and she justifies this assertion with pious cant – 'very serious
child protection issues' are at stake, their 'exploitation' cynical. Miss Widdecombe, her well-fed shadow, does not trouble
with such specious niceties and so obviously relishes her role as
the Conservative Party's Cruella de Vil that she has become the
Spitting Image puppet of herself. Both women are inspired by
Jack Straw with his recurrent condemnation of beggars on the
Underground.

What is the point of their litanies of opprobrium against
these wretched souls if it is not to whip the electorate into a
fever of hatred? Shall we, at the next election, find that the
major parties in their manifestos vie with promises to expel
these hapless families on the grounds that they don't know how
to behave on the streets of what Tony Blair once described as our
'decent, civic society', that they are spongers, bums, parasites
and scum, here only to exploit our generosity, their applications
for asylum bogus?

Blair was then the Leader of the Opposition, but he set the tone
for Straw and Roche with his attitude to the English homeless
who were driven to beg, speaking of them in January 1997 with
the immaculate heartless complacency of the authentic middle-
class Protestant Christian, offering 'hard-headed compassion',
preaching Zero Tolerance for the Barbarians, and proud to tell
us that he never gives to beggars.

I asked him then if he had ever come into direct contact
with the homeless on the South Bank (since purged), in the
underground passages at Hyde Park Corner, in the shop

doorways of the Strand, and I ask now if the smug Straw, complacent Roche and ranting Widdecombe have ever seen the mendicants from Kosovo, Albania and Romania on their home territory, if they know what it is to have to patch the patches on a pair of trousers, what it is to own nothing, what it is to be a gipsy anywhere in Europe, considered alien and rootless in a continent where borders are political and every man must have a passport and be of acceptable ethnic origin.

For the very poor of Eastern Europe the last honest resort is begging, and that is precisely what they do when they are destitute – better to sing a plaintive folk song to the unseeing faces on the District Line than to pick pockets. Where they come from, imploring charity is not a crime, and I have never seen a policeman in Istanbul, Tirana, Pristina, Prague, Warsaw or Moscow kick a beggar off the street. But here I have seen one seize a beggar's child and roughly hustle it away, a frantic parent screaming in his wake – not a sight that made me proud to be an Englishman.

These people are not criminals in any sense that I acknowledge; nor, alas, are they refugees in the strict sense of suffering well-founded fear of persecution; no one has attached electrodes to their genitals, repeatedly put their heads in buckets of water or accused them of political subversion, but it would be better if they had, for then these wretches would fall within the definition and we would welcome them. No – these are the 'bogus asylum seekers' of Jack Straw's disfavour, his 'economic migrants', attracted here, not by the myth of our welcome to Kossuth and Garibaldi, but by the Chinese whispers of our charity, the homes, the help, the health and education that we give to everybody destitute.

The system is at fault; the Conservatives were first to blame, but New Labour has been at least as complacent, indolent and indecisive; the Home Office has for donkey's years been staffed by purblind and indolent civil servants who should have foreseen the problem and prepared for it; the immigration authorities have long proved themselves incompetent; and the fathers of the church are more concerned with Clause 28 than with Christian charity.

We like having the odd politician here as an asylum seeker, the odd outspoken journalist, the odd Left-wing Chilean or Right-wing Russian – asylum for these reminds us of our great days under Gladstone and Disraeli, makes us feel good and generous and liberal – but we don't want the ragged poor of Europe's stinking underbelly, we don't want bloody gipsies with their snotty brats, and if we catch them begging then it's up before the magistrates and onto the new 'fast track' that sends them whence they came.

Not a bad idea, this fast track – the law employed to camouflage our racial prejudice, a useful instrument to prove that the scapegoat has only himself to blame for his expulsion. I am old enough to remember how often I heard 'Bloody Jew' said in queues for rationed food, how I, too, said it in a school that had its share of bergs and steins, and now I hear the sentiment again in conversation, on the radio and television, in the weasel words of Straw and Roche, in the strident calls of cold-eyed Widdecombe, and I am ashamed.

Let me remind these harsh politicians of the inscription on the Statue of Liberty:

> *'Give me your tired, your poor,*
> *Your huddled masses yearning to breathe free,*
> *The wretched refuse of your teeming shore,*
> *Send them, the homeless, tempest-tossed, to me...'*

ADDICTION
11 APRIL 2000

Drugs damage minds, break up families, perpetuate a despairing underclass and subvert human dignity – so said the *Daily Mail* when the Police Federation report on drugs was published last month. *The Times* said much the same, but with admirable brevity – 'Drugs ruin lives' was the editor's conclusion. And so they do, say I, victim of one of them, knowing that were it subject to the same prohibitions as those marketed by drug barons, it would ruin mine.

I took to it in my early teens and almost at once became dependent on it. Two years of National Service cut short the addiction, the pain of deprivation hardly noticed when basic army training inflicted so many other pains, but as a student I willingly returned to my enslavement and have ever since been subjugated by it.

I need to feel this drug coursing through my veins, responding with exultation to the renewal of my physical and intellectual energy. In the early morning I cannot begin to function without a shot of it, and throughout the day the drip-feed of controlled doses maintains its high level of activity.

Occasionally I take an overdose, an accidental excess of it, the consequences a racing pulse, nausea, trembling hands, headaches, depression and the jitters, and to these the only effective response is withdrawal. But the symptoms caused by depriva-

ADDICTION

tion are much the same as those of excess, and I am left weak
and drained, an empty husk until I take another dose of it – and
then the rush of exhilaration, as once again I feel alive, makes
the cycle of excess and denial utterly inevitable.

My cardiologist insists that I must break my habit. I fret
about palpitations and he tells me that I know the cure; I com-
plain that my heart feels like the single-cylinder diesel engine
of a Turkish fishing boat, my pacemaker like the turbo of an
early Saab, and his dour response is that I know the remedy;
I grumble that nausea overwhelms me, that I feel faint, that
sleep is wakeful, that my bladder has the capacity of a tennis
ball, and he shakes his head in bored despair. 'It is killing you,'
he says, 'give it up.'

I cannot. I have tried, time and again, but I cannot free
myself from an addiction that has as firm a hold on me as
heroin, cocaine or crack. My drug is not recreational, not
taken to heighten the pleasure of the dance, not a popper to
extend the sexual experience, not E or LSD, not a narcotic nor
a sedative. It is not sold at the school gates by seedy whites in
grubby anoraks, nor by dapper blacks in BMWs; it is not in the
gift of adolescent friends at raves and concerts; it is available
in every supermarket, every high street, every village shop. It is
caffeine.

I do not care whether it is ground from the five-year-old
bean of far Sumatra, subtle and pale from such long loitering,
or from the dark roast of Mocha; I do not care whether it is in
granules, Mr Nestlé's blended with gold dust and the pubic clip-
pings of Norwegian blondes, or Lord Sainsbury's very own and
unadorned; I do not care if it is an espresso as black as a Nubian
scrotum or the breakfast cafe latte to be had on Como's shores.

I care only that my coffee has not been decaffeinated and
gives me the required kick. If it does not, then out comes

125

the snuff box, not for a snort, but for the boost of Nescafé. My friends have seen me scatter it on a cappuccino, thicken an espresso, darken a *cafe filtre*, add it to a glass of Coca-Cola and spoon the dramatically rising froth; they have seen me, in extremis, place it on my tongue and let saliva do the work; those who have trekked and climbed with me have seen it mixed with muesli, yoghurt, honey and snow.

I am an addict. The Chancellor could punitively tax it, as he does tobacco, and I would pay the price, or smuggle it tucked in my underpants, or buy it from menacing dealers on the corners of Old Compton Street. Tony Blair could preach another sermon and appoint another Tsar, but I'd not care a damn and ask my friends from foreign parts to play bootlegger with it. The Archbishop of Canterbury could declare it sinful, quoting the authority of Paul and Habakkuk, but I'd raise my middle finger to him yet again. I am an addict and I will not, cannot, do without my coffee.

As an addict, I have some sympathy with those addicted to far stronger stuff. I have friends who cannot function without alcohol and nicotine, whose dependence must be satisfied with the first waking breath of day, and who, to pay the price decided on in Downing Street, cut back on other things. I have a friend with multiple sclerosis for whom, as Beta Interferon is denied him (too far gone, they say), illegal cannabis affords relief and he quite rightly buys it, but at crippling expense.

I have talked to young men and women addicted to cocaine and heroin who sustain their habits by prostitution, shoplifting and theft from cars, of which the insurance, police and prison costs must be incalculably large. The Police Federation report estimates that the illegal international trade in drugs in worth not less than £1,000 billion a year and possibly three times that figure. In Britain, annually, some 100,000 arrests are made for possession of cannabis, ecstasy and LSD – think of the cost of that in police time. Some 500,000 use ecstasy every weekend and get away with it.

There is now widespread belief that the Government's repressive policies cannot work and that we should at least be more permissive with recreational drugs. Let me suggest a more radical response. Let us take the profit out of illegal drugs by making them all legal. Let the addict walk into any pharmacy and pick up a clean needle and a measured dose of heroin or crack for much the same as it costs to buy a ticket on a London bus. With no law broken, there will be no consequent adrenal thrill, no one to whom to sell drugs for a profit, no point in stealing a car radio, no point in shoplifting or prostitution, and cannabis can grow on the kitchen window-sill. No addict need die of a contaminated dose nor contract HIV from an infected needle; no MS sufferer will feel compelled to affect innocence in his wheelchair when he spies PC Plod.

With such freedom from drug barons and prosecution, there may well be fewer addicts and certainly fewer accidental deaths, and it is probable that with a government and all authority seeming utterly indifferent to our shooting, snorting and guzzling drugs, our experimental appetite for them would fade, and only a small band of inadequates (like the poor, always with us) would continue on their way, as irredeemable as smokers, boozers, wine-bibbers and coffee-drinkers – which means almost every adult in the British Isles. We are all addicted to something – some of us to the power-piety of imposing abstention on others.

A WEEKEND IN
THE COUNTRY
25 APRIL 2000

It has recently been my misfortune to spend a few days in the country – though that is perhaps better expressed as a few days in the provinces and better still as in provincial towns with nothing of Turgenev about them. I was drawn thither by the promise of substantial art galleries and all the notable monuments and buildings usually associated with a history dating back to the Dark Ages, about which guide books and tourist boards invariably lie, and by the attraction if the unknown. 'Keep England for your old age,' said my step-father many years ago, a man whom the First World War had sent to Mesopotamia, Jerusalem and the wilds to the north of Salonika, and thus it is that to me the stews of Istanbul and the ancient churches of Armenia are more familiar than the cathedral cities of this country. I have followed the Via Egnatia from Rome to Byzantium and trodden the impulsive wayward route of Alexander from Troy to Issus, every step of it, but have never set foot on Offa's Dyke or Hadrian's Wall and know nothing of the delights of towns in which the Great Eliza may have burnt a cake, or the Great Alfred slept with Ealswitha, siring King Edward.

Alas, in my brief search for the authentic England I did not discover it. It is true that I found rampart walls, but these were as discontinuous as the tooth stumps of a tobacco-chewing seaman accustomed to biting the necks of beer bottles. It is true that I found fine gothic churches, but their doors were locked, no candles guttered and no boy sopranos sang. It is true that I found fine houses built by merchants with a merry trade in slaves and the works of slavery, but their Erne classical facades were marred by the vulgar corporate insignia of building societies and banks. It is true that I found byways and backwaters of pedestrianised conservation, but these were self-consciously neat, clean, re-processed and deprived of meaning, reduced to the authenticity of ornaments advertised in Sunday supplements as limited editions and bought for her mantelpiece by Hyacinth Bucket. But authentic English hospitality and food I failed to find, or failed to recognise.

What did I expect? The cherubic smile of doormen in top hats, a flurry of footmen to carry my bags, fresh fruit and the fizzy widow waiting in my room? Well no, not in the dark provinces – but something that made me feel a little welcome and less like a battery hen destined for its doom. For £99 a night what does one get in provincial England? – a building that in its cheap and bleak design (it cannot be called architecture) is as hostile to the soul as a block of workman's flats on the outskirts of Zagreb.

To the dyed blonde behind the desk I was the 500th client of the day and she was not about to crack the plaster of her make-up with a smile; nor, on a wet and windy night, was there a lusty boy to help me lug my luggage to the lift, let alone to the umpteenth floor and past the trays of discarded chips and desiccated sandwiches, cold teapots and mucilaginous plates with which the corridor was littered.

In my room, at last, I found a window that 'in the interests of child safety' could be opened only an inch, and that at the top, so that only a Force 10 gale head on could force fresh air into the drab brown box that was to be my home for a night or two. There was no wardrobe – only an open rail; nor was there a chest of drawers; the fridge was stuffed with drinks at precisely five times the supermarket price; and, measured to the milligram, there was enough Nescafe and everlasting milk to make one cup and a half of reasonable coffee – for £99 how could an hotel be so mean? The one luxurious note was the large television set on which, for a fee, one was able to watch pornography selected by the management – odd how we close down Soho and prohibit kerb-crawling but encourage Mondeo-men to masturbate in our hotels.

Dinner in such establishments is served by untrained children who hardly know fork from spoon and the explicitly descriptive menus mislead utterly; prune Archangelic halibut, pale as a maiden's inner thigh, reclining on a bed of caramelised violets, served with seaweed crisped in Oil of Ulay, reaches the table as a chunk of white rubber in primeval ooze. The ubiquitous McDonald's is next door, and one step up from it is TGI Friday's, staffed by terrified mutant bunny-girls with fluffy tails sprouting from their shoulder blades, where wild Antarctic salmon is lovingly seared with sticks of glowing charcoal by thigh-looted, whip-cracking kitchen maids specially for you-hoo; in such a place the simple refreshment of a plain vanilla ice cannot be had – one must choose a Chocolate Chunky Monkey or a Strapping Strawberry Wench.

These provincial dinners are not cheap – indeed one could eat well for less in Launceston Place or Brown's Hotel – and much of the disgusting food is left uneaten on the plate. The alternatives are take-aways, Chinese, Indian and Thai, or old pubs themed to match new names, the Fag and Carrot, Condom and Firkin, offering dead sausages and pie-fillings of dung and Bisto.

A WEEKEND IN THE COUNTRY

In what now lies the Englishness of England? In its countryside, stripped of wood and copse, naked of hedgerow, where no birds sing? In its country towns, fringed with estates of little boxes built by property developers contemptuous of the local architectural vernacular? In its cities, victims of concrete rising high, every inch a rental fortune for its alien masters? In its local customs, local culture, local food? There may be an identifiable Scottishness in Scotland and a Welshness in Wales to justify their devolution, but in England there is no Englishness to warrant an English parliament. Whatever once was Englishness – Hearts of Oak, Gilbert and Sullivan, and There'll always be an England set in a silver sea – is now swamped by gross commercialism, curry and the ghastly multiculturalism that has nothing in it of any true identity and is an all-consuming sludge.

I cannot understand how the nation's Tourist Board and the Ministry of Culture can be so dishonest as to urge any foreign visitor to venture beyond the Inner Circle. Virtues discernible no longer in the shires are abundant still in London, and in spite of crowds, noise and congestion, fast food, litter and a public transport system run by neglectful idiots, it is still a great city, still lively in spite of the Westminster councillors who try to neuter it, still wonderful and beautiful in spite of lordly architects. It deserves a mayor who will fight tooth and nail for it and damn the politics of Parliament. Damn the amorphous mess that is the rest of England too – give London devolution, for she houses, when all is said and done, as many souls as the lands of the leek and the kilt together. A pox on being lumped with Birmingham and Manchester and Liverpool too, the whining Sodoms and Gomorrahs of the north.

131

PORNOGRAPHY
13 JUNE 2000

At what age should children be exposed to pornography? I ask the question because an attempt by the British Board of Film Classification to censor pornographic videos that are readily available all over Europe and North America, was recently overturned by its own Video Appeals Committee. Alarmed by such an excess of liberalism, the Board took to the law to appeal against the appeal, its counsel pleading that it is unseemly, improper, indecent, offensive and corrupting for children to be the spectators at scenes of coitus and masturbation, but in vain, for the judge ruled in favour of the Appeals Committee. Both sides seem to have agreed that vivid pornography for adults is already so available here, illegally, that there can be no further harm in permitting its sale in licensed sex shops, releasing customs and police officers for altogether duller duties. The argument, therefore, centred on children's accidental access to it and whether they might be harmed by chance exposure, and both the Appeals Committee and the learned judge took the view that harm to children could be more or less discounted – hence my asking at what age a child may learn to take scenes of foreplay and coitus in his stride.

Many parents in our society seem to be so alarmed by their children's sexuality that they occlude both it and memories of their own infant and adolescent experience, their determination to maintain the myth of wholesome innocence compelling children to recognise that sexual pleasure is not a suitable subject for enquiry. My recollection of sex education at school, delivered by a cassocked chaplain, is that pleasure was never mentioned, though gasping with pleasure was pretty well all we knew about it; this godly man outlined the mechanics of reproduction, attributed erection to some mysterious response to cerebral stimulus without which procreation could not take place, condemned self-abuse and likened a wet dream to clearing blocked pipes below the kitchen sink; with marriage, we were assured, something wonderful would happen, but we knew not what.

All this we solemnly accepted as we did the mortise and tenon joint in woodwork, but we knew that pleasure, not procreation, was the driving force in our sexual activity. We were fiercely curious and greedy for a sight of anything that might qualify, in effect, as pornographic, though how the neutered and depilated nudes of *Health and Efficiency*, could have excited us so much now seems astonishing. We were hungry for knowledge and the worse for being deprived of it. We knew nothing of women's pleasure, nor of their masturbation – indeed, without a penis, how could it be possible? – for clitoris was not a word that had passed the chaplain's lips. We knew nothing of fetishes, though some of us already had them – basketball boots, belts, favourite pairs of rugger or athletic shorts, jockstraps, cricket boxes, even a bicycle inner tube – and feared the embarrassment of their discovery; now we know that they are commonplace, encouraged by therapists and marriage guidance counsellors, and in all sorts of absurd forms to be bought by anyone bold enough to enter a sex shop, or through the post by shy readers of the *Daily Telegraph* on Saturdays. My generation of boys got their illicit thrill from the mere mention of Lady Chatterley, though we never knew for certain what Mellors did to her, any more than we knew what really happened in Henry Miller's Tropics, and the wild imaginings of an adolescent, wholly uninformed, were possibly more dangerous and desperate than the blaséness of teenagers now who, surfeited, know exactly how sodomy, fellatio and cunnilingus are performed.

It is not without wry amusement that we picture Mr Justice Hooper, the board, the committee, their counsel and solicitors solemnly inspecting every scene of *Nympho Nurse Nancy*. The title tells all – of nurse and uniform fetishes, of Nancy with the consultant surgeon and the weary houseman, of Nancy adjusting the traction of a helpless patient with a multiplicity of broken bones, of Nancy with the sturdy porter and the boilerman, and in all the other couplings implied by nymphomania in a hospital. Ban this, they thought, and where does the banning stop? Where indeed, for if such videos must be forbidden, what do we do about the printed page and works of art? We cannot return to the dreadful days of the Lady Chatterley trial and the police raid on the Aubrey Beardsley exhibition at the V&A.

Consider what is to be seen in the Tate Modern now; consider the explicit sex and vernacular language of the contemporary novel; consider the current list of the Benedikt Taschen press, publishers of fine and serious books on art, design, style and photography. In this last we find *Erotica Universalis*, the Latin title offering respectability to a quick-flick picture history of coupling from far antiquity to Madame La Bondage in the Fifties and Tom of Finland in the Eighties. Those with a taste for Tom, if they look a little further, will find that Taschen has taken this bull by the horn and published the bumper book for boys, an album called The Art of Pleasure (pleasure? – there's daring), with all the conventions of the leatherman drawn large. In the elegant, detached, observant photography

PORNOGRAPHY

of Roy Stuart and Natacha Merritt we have the images of the top-shelf magazine mysteriously lifted to a higher plane, the subjects and activities identical but, to borrow Miss Merritt's words, taking pornographic photographs is for her '… a way to exhibit love, and engage with her lover, a reason to explore and experiment'. It is in this involvement that the distinction lies; the photographs of Merritt and Stuart may not quite be art, but they are certainly not the pornography of the sex shop; to boys of my generation, puzzled by oncoming puberty, they would have been wonderful sources of information,

If the BBC can broadcast as family entertainment a soap episode on the subject of a video tape devoted to lesbians and spanking (2 June), I cannot see the point of a Classification Board that seeks to prevent us from seeing such a tape. The genie is now out of the bottle here, and in northern Europe, where it has never been in the bottle, there is no evidence of harm to either adults or children. Adults must be allowed to see what they choose, and if they shun pornography, as I shun caviar, foie gras, veal and other cruelties to animals for their obscenity, that is their choice; they may seek to influence me, as I seek to influence them, but only with reasoned argument, not with hypocrisy, bigotry and prohibition. It is the responsibility of parents, not the law, to determine when their children come to terms with the adult world, and for that the most sensitive preparation is to make them understand that coitus is a matter of exquisite pleasure, a thousand times more often than of pro-creation. In that pleasure and its associated stimuli, diversions and substitutes, provided that partners are willing, they should feel no guilt. It is guilt that does the damage, not pornography.

BIBLE STORIES
31 OCTOBER 2000

Were I a Jew whose parents had reached Israel when it was still a promised land in the immediate aftermath of the Holocaust and the Second World War, I have no doubt that I would defend my stripling country with the same strenuous fervour as the Likud Party, the Israeli army and police now do, the Old Testament my romantic justification. Had I been born a Palestinian, my parents deprived of hereditary land, driven back into the Gaza strip that was once the territory of ancient Philistines, cut off from the Holy Places of Islam, denied education, medicine, hope, I have equally no doubt that I would be as frustrated and enraged at my virtual imprisonment in the Third World as any young man in Gaza now, and that I too would be out on the streets with stones in hand, perhaps even driven to lynch if the opportunity occurs.

It is all very well for us, by which I mean the Americans, the Norwegians (who now can recall the Oslo agreement?), the European Union and the United Nations, as well as the British – to prate of talk to both these parties, as though in protracted discussion they can be so ground down to exhaustion that they will agree to sleep in the same bed. Their talking leaders might, briefly. There was evidence of this in the body language of Arafat and Barak when President Clinton had them locked away for day-after-day discussion in a 'peace process' in America

– but in truth it was a process less of peace than of fraudulent self-deception that could never be sustained after their return to their respective 'real worlds' in Gaza and Jerusalem. Even if, for a while, they could have maintained the fiction for themselves, the grudging suspicion that each had come back from Munich, as it were, clutching a worthless piece of paper, that each had betrayed his cause, would eventually have eroded any agreement they had seemed to reach, the erosion hastened by supporters who had not suffered the exhaustion of talk, talk among the lavish comforts of America, but been at home amid the Sturm und Drang, perhaps even deliberately worsening the situation.

At best, the Israelis are prepared to tolerate a toothless Palestine, a Palestine that offers no military or economic threat, a Palestine that will always be, cap-in-hand and underclass, a client state, its claims to the sacred sites of Jerusalem, a holy city of Islam, denied. At worst, we should not doubt that there are Israelis who, setting aside the lessons of the Holocaust, see ethnic cleansing as the one permanent answer, another Bosnia, another Kosovo, three million worthless peasants of Islam wiped out, the suppurating boil lanced once and for all, the integrity of the Holy Land from Dan to Beersheba and beyond secured in such a way that no new Assyrian, Egyptian, Roman or Christian – and certainly no Philistine – would ever seek to breach it.

Were this last course to be pursued, its apologists would argue that America, largely unwillingly perhaps, would contrive to support Israel – as it has in every diplomatic crunch – because neither Democrat nor Republican can afford to alienate the domestic Jewish vote, and with America as ally, Israel is safe. And perhaps she is; her leaders could behave as badly as the war criminals of Yugoslavia and the Arab states on Israel's borders would yet again do nothing, would yet again leave the

Palestinians to fight alone, unaided and virtually unarmed. The Director of Excavations for the Palestine Exploration Fund who wrote in 1911 that in Palestine 'the Arab will remain master at the end, as he was in the beginning', was in grave error.

Was the Arab there in the beginning? Was the Jew? Did Palestine ever have borders until we, the British, traced lines in the sand after the First World War, claiming a mandate there to protect our routes to India and the oil wells of Iraq? Whatever Palestine was in our imaginations a century and more ago when we were covertly establishing ourselves through antiquarian, archaeological and Biblical enquiry, when we hoped that by making it a Church of England Bishopric it would become a converted Christian Holy Land, it was not a Jewish homeland but part of the Ottoman Empire, occupied by far more Arabs than Jews and a stronghold of Islam. In early Biblical times, it lay on the trade routes of ancient Egypt, Persia, the Hittites, with whom Abraham did business, and the civilisations of the Tigris and Euphrates; under such international pressures, could it ever have been as exclusively Jewish as the Bible implies? The New Testament gives the impression of an entirely Jewish satrapy, but when the Crusades began a millennium later, they were fought against Arabs and Islam, with hardly a Jew in evidence. Under the Turks, Palestine was remarkable for long centuries of peace, and might well still be so had it not been for the Balfour Declaration of 1917.

By the Balfour Declaration Britain was committed to the notion of an ancestral home for the Jews in Palestine. It was an utterly cynical propaganda ploy to bring into alliance with the British in the First World War the mythical great force (in terms of wealth and political influence) of International Jewry. It took the form of a letter from Lord Balfour, the Foreign Secretary, to Lord Rothschild, a prominent Zionist; it offered no secure guarantees to the existing population; it was used as our reason for demanding the post-war Mandate; and it was the cause of bitter argument until, in a welter of violence from Jewish terrorists, we abandoned the territory to the United Nations in 1948.

If we are now appalled by the Palestinian lynching of Jewish soldiers, we should not forget that in July 1947, Jewish terrorists abducted two British sergeants, hanged them and booby-trapped their bodies. We should not forget the atrocity of 91 deaths when the so-called National Military Organisation dynamited offices of the Mandate in the King David Hotel in 1946. We have much to remember of Irgun and the Israel Freedom Fighters.

'Without the Balfour Declaration we would not have had the Mandate; without the Mandate we would not have had the British administration; without the British administration … the Jewish presence in Palestine would not have developed into a threat to our existence … and our political rights.' These were the words of a Palestinian diplomat 25 years ago and they are a just indictment still; I have borrowed them from *Ploughing Sand*, Naomi Shepherd's remarkable book on British rule in Palestine (John Murray, 1999) – essential reading, as reviewers used to say.

To the onlooker, it seems that, while the rest of us must constantly be reminded of the Holocaust, build museums and memorials to it, carry guilt for it from generation to generation and flagellate our consciences, the Israeli Jews can behave as unacceptably to native Palestinians as other nations have to minorities in their midst. If ever there were an instrument of International Jewry, it is the exploitation of the Holocaust to neuter opposition from the reasonable man. If America stopped believing that what happens in Israel influences the domestic politics of the United States, Israelis might feel compelled to confront the need that all western nations face – the need, by force of circumstances, to become a multicultural society. And the rest of us must stop believing as a sentimental article of faith the distorted history promoted by the Bible.

FISHING
14 NOVEMBER 2000

A week ago, on the south-west corner of Australia, in three fathoms of water off a beach that looks directly across the Indian Ocean to Cape Province, a middle-aged man with a moustache, balding and bespectacled, taking an early-morning dip was bitten by a great white shark. Wry Edward Lear might well have amused us with a limerick illustrated by a caricature – an alternative version, perhaps of 'There was an old man of the South/Who had an immoderate mouth ...', with, in this case the shark as the immoderately proportioned party; it bit off one leg, found the crunch and texture not to its taste and swam away, leaving the man, poor soul, to die of immoderate exsanguinations, watched by friends in a nearby cafe who were quite put off their breakfast of bacon and black pudding. News of the death was wired to London for the delectation of broadsheet editors who gave us full-face photographs of both a great white shark and the late Mr Crew, with the unfortunate man looking much less agreeable, his death described as tragedy.

A tragedy? A tragedy is surely some personal catastrophe that destroys the life or reputation of a man who has some claim to greatness, an event that echoes in our minds for centuries, that carries an ethical lesson from one generation to another, that crosses the boundaries of culture and is the stuff of allegory and drama; tragedy, whatever its form stirs the spirit or leaves a lasting mark on our morality. The loss of one human being of whom none of us have ever heard, is a mere mishap, not a tragedy, an event of no importance made famous in the 15-minute Warhol sense by the guignol of the shark.

If tragedy there were to be in this event, it could lie only in the death of the shark. The great white is, fortunately, a protected species under Australian law, to be killed only as a last resort and with permission, but the permission was immediate and police marksmen hanging out of helicopters at once began the chase, reflecting the prompt demand for vengeance and the need to keep our beaches safe. Our beaches? Safe for whom or what? Must the pleasure of man always have primacy? What is safety when dolphins, porpoises and manatees carry the scars of outboard engines and often die of such wounds? Water is their only habitat, it must be emphasised, yet even in the most frivolous particular we demand supremacy and its acknowledgement by animals. Great white sharks, however, are not known for intellectual debate or encyclopaedic knowledge and a man dog-paddling in their environment is merely another form of prey, there to be eaten, not a partner with whom to discuss the moral maze. The great white shark is an endangered species, we are not; all shark populations are declining, some species by 80 per cent, hunted for meaningless sport, caught for their fins to satisfy Far Eastern diets and, utterly disabled without them, thrown back into the sea to die. It may be the most marvellous of nature's predators, but it is no match for greedy, thoughtless, selfish men.

And we are greedy, thoughtless and selfish. Among this autumn's crop of headlines is 'Cull may spell end for the dolphin', topping the tale of the Japanese fishermen who annually drive these intelligent creatures into the trap of narrow inlets, hook them from the water and then stab them so that they slowly bleed to death. Even Elliot Morley, Minister and apologist for MAFF, our ghastly government department of agriculture and fisheries, a man wholly indifferent to the export of live animals and the dreadful deaths of cattle, sheep and pigs in our abattoirs, felt compelled to describe the dolphin slaughter as '…a bloodbath…a scene from a horror movie'. Dolphins die so that we may eat their flesh in fashionable restaurants as sushi – 22,000 of them in the coastal traps this year, with a further 17,000 harpooned in open waters; the catch is entirely uncontrolled, occurs every year and is resulting in the near extinction of the rarer species. In 1986 the Japanese corralled so many dolphins that the sushi trade could not absorb them; the superfluous catch was not released but fed, head first and still alive, into the mincing machines that reduce waste fish to agricultural fertiliser. Since seeing that I have refused all invitations to Japan and events Japanese, and have been accused of 'Japan bashing' in reviews and articles.

The Japanese attitude is that the last elephant will die before they stop carving their beastly netsuke in ivory, the last whale – which they hunt voraciously – will die before they relinquish its meat from their diet (and now the dolphin too), and that nature is there to be bent to man's will. Perhaps we should not be quite so ready with harsh judgement when we learn that the performing dolphins that so amuse us in the dolphinariums of western holiday resorts go blind because they always face the sun, so that we can better see them leap and grin and dance on the water. Should we not be sickened to learn that the Thai Elephant Conservation Centre has had to raise funds by forming an Elephant Orchestra to entertain mindless tourists with performances on drums and xylophone? How can we criticise the Japanese when the oh-so-civilised Danes of the EU massacre a thousand pilot whales on the Faroe Islands every year. Whole families are wiped out even to the last pregnant female, in much the same way as the Japanese with their dolphins, indiscriminately, uncontrolled and cruelly violent, the sea frothing red with blood, the filthy business justified as a cultural tradition. And what of the tuna fishermen of Sicily? There's a spectacle vile enough to turn a man's stomach from ever eating tuna.

I could go on and on. Man's greed and selfishness have made a wasteland of the North Sea and a delicacy of cod and skate, haddock and monkfish, once the commonplaces of the cat, the poor, the breakfast and the Friday fast, but now all on the menus of expensive restaurants. It is man's obstinate thoughtlessness, no more than that, that compels the Muslims and the Jews to slaughter animals for meat by exsanguination fully conscious, without the benefit of stunning – but any comment in those quarters is always damned as cultural prejudice.

It is man's beastliness here, in England, that leads him to mistreat farm animals in market places (the ministry's reports are there to prove it), in transit and in abattoirs, and we have very little in the matter of animal welfare of which we can be proud. Consider these recently published observations from a vet employed to see that all is well in abattoirs – '…all cattle over 30-months are slaughtered and most are pregnant dairy cows … when these creatures are hanging on the line bleeding to death you can see the unborn calves kicking in their mothers' wombs. I, as a vet, am not supposed to do anything about this. Unborn calves don't exist, according to regulations … and no one seems to care.'

Ken Crew was not a tragic victim, but every shark, dolphin, porpoise, turtle, tiger, leopard, lynx, whale, rhinoceros and bear killed by man now is, each wanton death bringing the extinction of the species a step nearer. There are countless millions of us,

FISHING

nobodies all, yet it is we who have become the inexorable force that overwhelms the animal victim, that inflicts the extinction that is true tragedy, and our souls are numbed and sullied by every act of cruelty that is the beginning of this end.

BEAR BAITING
15 JANUARY 2001

I have no happy memories of Pakistan. Its cities are unmatched for traffic pollution and the contamination of garbage. In town and country abject poverty is ever-present, men, women and children, if not homeless, then cruelly enslaved in back-breaking toil that puts the meanest of roofs over their heads. And everywhere there is cruelty to animals, casual starvation, merciless overloading and vicious, spiteful beating of all beasts of burden, wanton indifference to what we think of as affectionate pets, and the brutal exploitation of anything wild that can be caught and abused for entertainment.

I remember a boy with a withered right arm begging by the roadside in the chill mists that hang on the Lowari Pass at 10,000ft or so, for he perfectly symbolised the hopelessness of the Pakistani poor and the futility of my wanting to do something, anything, to help. And I remember too the pelican tethered outside a medicine shop in Chitral; it may have had some token meaning there, its more interesting parts the source of primitive remedies – I do not know – I know only that down among the traffic fumes, pinioned and filthy, de-prived of water, its constant preening desperate, it was another cause of anguish. My companions dragged me away from its misery – 'What,' they argued, 'can you do with a pelican that can no longer fly?'

146

BEAR BAITING

They had earlier dragged me away from a bleeding donkey in Peshawar. Not much more than a foal, loose amid the traffic, blood poured from four deep punctures in its back caused by projections from a wicker 'saddle' for its load. How could an owner wantonly inflict such pain? How could a sane man expect to get the best out of a beast so cruelly laden? But sanity and kindness play no part in animal husbandry in Pakistan. Even my friends felt that something had to be done when we came upon men kicking a fallen donkey that lay on its chest and belly, all four legs outstretched, under a formidable and uneven load of timber. Unable to regain purchase with any hoof it lay there and endured. We removed its load, lifted it to its feet, calmed it and, with heavy heart, reloaded it; I have no doubt that as soon as they lost sight of us, the Pakistanis kicked it yet again.

By what, in last week's papers, I saw of bear-baiting in Pakistan, I was reminded of these, my lesser reasons for never returning to that benighted country. I have seen the pathetic dancing bears there and know the dilemma well – should we give the owners money in the hope that the sad creature will be fed and watered with some small part of it, or should we walk sternly past in the belief that by not parting with our cash the wretched business will end – but with what end for the bear? But with bear-baiting, the filthy recreation of a toothless, clawless, tethered bear set upon by dogs for the amusement of a crowd, there is no dilemma – it is, simply, wrong. Think about the agony of teeth and claws drawn sans anaesthetic, and then think about nostrils, cheeks and eyes torn from the bear by hard-jawed dogs, bred for the purpose. There are, it seems, rules to this sport and the bear is sometimes judged to have won the contest – but I doubt if he knows it and is consoled by it for his wounds, and no vet is there to stitch and bind them. I saw 'Protect the Snow Leopard' on a rusting sign near Dir, and 'World Wildlife Fund for Nature – Migratory Bird Conservation' on another in the foothills of the Hindu Kush, but I doubt if either admonition has the slightest effect on the 20 per cent of Pakistanis who have the benefit of formal education and can read them. As for the 80 per cent who are illiterate – how can we expect of them anything other than a primitive response to the primitive pleasure of tormenting animals? The Asiatic black bear may be a protected animal, it may, at an estimated 300 survivors, be on the brink of extinction, but this evidently matters not at all to the Pakistani authorities who make laws and then ignore them, when the public spectacle of the bears' destruction is at stake. It is the age-old problem of sport's supremacy; with the demand for them in the arenas of ancient Rome the Caspian tiger met extinction, with the demand for it in the arenas of Pakistan, the Asian bear too will be killed off.

How can we, in the West, influence the fate of the Asian bear? What could one solitary Englishman do were he to stray into such a circus as we saw in our newspapers last week? Nothing, of course, just as he could do nothing to stop a bullfight in Seville. But something, somehow, must be done, though it will not be done by a government that sells arms, armaments and aeroplanes to Pakistan. Do we even occupy the moral high ground in this matter? We relinquished bear-baiting only in 1835 and hunting with hounds is still with us for fox and deer; Prince Charles's latest exploit in the field is the gossip of the Pakistani super-rich, of whom there are surprisingly many. A Pakistani bear-baiter could point too to our coursing hares with greyhounds, and were he to look into our husbandry of animals, what then would he see? He would see thousands of wild New Forest ponies sold, often for as little as £1, to French gluttons for horse flesh, brutally ill-treated from the moment of their capture until death greets them in a distant abattoir.

BEAR BAITING

He would see us callously exporting sheep for clumsy slaughter by French Muslims in the celebration of Eid-El-Kebir, see geese and ducks with funnels down their throats to make foie gras, see millions of pheasants fall to earth blasted with lead shot, see thousands of badgers killed in the misbegotten supposition that this will eliminate TB in cattle. He would see sows in farrowing crates and hens cramped in battery cages; he would, indeed, see millions of animals in cages, from the ape to the mouse, the subjects of vivisection, often for no medical purpose and grotesquely inappropriate; and he might wonder, having seen Sicilians kill tuna and Norwegians kill whales, that any man could eat the flesh of creatures so cruelly despatched.

The Lofoten islanders are as protected by the Norwegian authorities as are the Pakistani bear-baiters by theirs. Punjabi bear-baiting is a sport preserved by rich, virtually feudal landowners with such friends in the police, army and government that they are above the law, the sport an aspect of their superior status. The World Society for the Protection of Animals (WSPA) has, at the request of the Pakistani government, established a 12-acre sanctuary with a veterinary clinic for rescued bears, and will provide transport and fuel to carry any animal to it from anywhere in the country – but not one bear has yet been confiscated from the baiters. The sport has been illegal since 1998 and we can only conclude that it continues with the support of corruption, the indolence of bureaucrats and the powerful disinclination of the filthy rich to relinquish one of the means by which they retain their hold on an ignorant and primitive populace. We must point the finger at Raees Abbas Zaidi, who rejoices in the Gilbert and Sullivan title of additional secretary, and who admits that 'the local police are ineffective (and)… a purchasable commodity'.

A PRINCELY EDUCATION
11 SEPTEMBER 2001

Prince William is soon to become an undergraduate. He has learned to hunt, shoot and play polo; he has endured his share of mildly adventurous exploration and the minor hardships that must be suffered when this is done under watchful supervision; and he has spent some years at Eton, no doubt experiencing boyish pains and pleasures there as well as acquiring education enough to gain access to a university. We perhaps expected him to make for Oxford or Cambridge and work for a conventional degree in history or English, philosophy or economics. We perhaps thought that he might 'make a statement' by preferring some more obviously egalitarian seat of learning, Salford or Hull, or some metamorphosed polytechnic, the South Bank or Thames Valley universities, and pursue the 'vocational' subjects, such as computer science or hotel management (vocation in my youth meant medicine or the priesthood, eheu, eheu). But no, he chose the University of St Andrews on the wild and windy coast of Fife, with art history as his subject.

Art history? To those who are not art historians, history of art is an altogether less confusing term, for that is what this course of study is. It is not an easy option – or so I thought until I made enquiries. It may once, in this country, have been regarded as a suitable subject for well-bred girls as an alternative to finishing school, but Anthony Blunt put an end to that when he turned the Courtauld Institute into a monkish seminary and imbued his novices with unremitting fervour for the study. In Blunt's hands the history of art became the academic discipline of impeccable severity that it had been in Germany since 1844, when the first professorial chair was established in Berlin (Prince Albert of Saxe-Coburg-Gotha would have been proud of his great-great-great-great grandson for taking up Kunstgeschichte), but there were far earlier manifestations, the earliest the elder Pliny's observations on painting and sculpture 2,000 years ago, which in turn indicate the existence of still earlier treatises, now lost.

The bare bones of art history are linear studies of painting, sculpture and architecture, the simple first-this-then-that sequence that connects the painted image on the flat gold ground to the bucket-and-slosh business of the contemporary abstract painter, the iconography of Christ crucified painted for the devout veneration of the peasantry, to the Mapplethorpe photograph of a naked male with another man's fist thrust into his anus. With experience, the student will recognise that the history of art is far from linear, that its threads are looped and tangled in cats' cradles that may never be undone, that it has always been affected by external forces of political and social history, that it is inseparable from monarchs, popes and despots, famine, plague and war, is inseparable from theological and philosophical debate, is inseparable from music, literature and the wider cultural background of its day; of all these the student must know as much as of his core subject.

The history of art is a discipline that constantly reminds its students of how little they know, and yet, because it so often opens doors to different arts and disciplines, it always inspires them to explore and remedy their ignorance. It is, nevertheless, a discipline in which the menace of narrow obsession is inherent, though perhaps less so at St Andrews than elsewhere.

The course there lasts for four years. New students are not specifically prepared for it, need know nothing of art history nor of essential background culture and may not even have a reasonable command of English. In an attempt to compare the requirements of my young day at the Courtauld with those of Prince William now, I probed a little further. 'What about the Bible? How can students recognise subjects and iconography without a working knowledge of the Old and New Testaments, the Apocrypha, the Golden Legend?' To this the professorial answer was: 'The Bible is a worrying problem – knowledge of it is not to be taken for granted.'

I enquired about classical mythology, Roman history, Ovid's *Metamorphoses* and other sources of the painter's imagery with primary and secondary meanings, and of these learned that the student may be utterly ignorant – 'We cope with the school leavers we get,' said the glum voice.

'What about languages?' I asked, recalling that I had been required to have Latin or Greek and at least the ability to read French, German and Italian; and to this came the answer that there are now enough books in English to make other languages superfluous. To my suggestion that to any student wishing to study Byzantine art a little Greek must be essential, came the response: 'We don't do Byzantium.'

St Andrews provides 'modules' on the Scottish house, Scottish furniture, Scottish photography, Scottish art and Scottish nationalism, contemporary Scottish painting and Thomas Chippendale and Scotland (that should lead to some interesting confusions among ignorant undergraduates), but it doesn't do Byzantium. Nor does it do classical art. 'Without a nodding acquaintance with European languages, how do your raw students pronounce the names of such painters as Cimabue, Pollaiuolo and Guercino, Runge, Schnorr and Baldung Grien?' I asked. 'Wrongly: we teach pronunciation as we go along.' 'Has Prince William a reading list with which to prepare for his first term?' – and to this the answer was that nothing particular is required. 'Students are much less prepared, nowadays.' 'Yes,' I muttered, 'and they need four years instead of three.'

In the first two years, Prince William will study survey courses on art in Renaissance Italy, European art and architecture of the 17th and 18th centuries, 19th century architecture and design, and the international modern movement 1905-1990. With only three lectures and one tutorial each week, the courses are broad in treatment and hardly arduous. Classes are 'enormous' – 150 in the first year, with tutorial groups of nine. In the third and fourth years the student must choose from 12, four 'honours modules' to study; these depend on the research interests of the staff and staff availability and willingness; they may be taught in any order, no matter how anachronical, ghastly Bellany before divine Bellini. 'We provide a smattering, an entree to the subject.'

With this I felt for a moment that we were back in the frivolity of the Thirties when the Courtauld Institute first opened its doors but closed them for Ascot week and debutantes' balls, as though Blunt, a decade or so later, had never transformed it from a finishing school into an academic faculty that was the envy of the world and one that did indeed 'do' Byzantium for undergraduates. How can this smattering, this entree, be a proper preparation for a first degree, let alone for research, a thesis and a higher degree or PhD? This dumbing down has indeed turned the history of art into an easy option – easier for Prince William than most if he has paid some small attention to his grandmama's collection of old masters. This degree might just prepare him for the job of charmer on the reception desk at Christie's, but not much more, unless the revolution comes and the New Labour state requires an authoritative guide to the people's collections in Buck House, Windsor Castle and, with so many useful Scottish 'modules', Balmoral as a subject of particular expertise.

AFGHANISTAN
16 OCTOBER 2001

Recalling the lies told us during the Falklands War, the tales of the pin-point accuracy of our bombardment of Iraqi cities and the mythology of missiles fired into the windows of Belgrade that then searched the corridors for precisely the right room in which to find Milosevic, many of us view the current devastation of Kabul and Kandahar with profound scepticism. We wonder, too, what advice Blair has been given by old hands at the Foreign Office and how much of it has been ignored by his close advisers in 10 Downing Street, those clever youngsters who theoretically know everything so much better. We wonder at the ease with which this demonstrably Christian man who has no experience of war, has never fought, never served in any sense, never as a civilian suffered its calamities, whose loudest bang has been a jolly firework, has embarked upon a war with what has some claim to be the poorest nation in the world. In a land never fertile and now impoverished by drought, a land in which the duvet is utterly unknown, a land in which the patches on old clothes are patched and patched again, a land where Islington's spoonful of polenta would be a luxury, the Afghans are a people not only widely illiterate, but so ignorant of the West and its troubles that they can have no concept of the terrorism of which Blair's complaint is the justification for his bombs and rockets.

Think on that. These people have no word for terrorism in their three main languages, no word for it in those small cultural pockets in which the Greek of Alexander the Great still echoes faintly, and as a concept in this merciless country it is inconceivable. Over the past two centuries or so, western travellers, soldiers and diplomats have invariably characterised the Afghan as quarrelsome, distrustful, unscrupulous, treacherous, turbulent, vindictive, suspicious, inured to bloodshed and capable of gross brutality, both recklessly and with calculated intent; these observers saw death inflicted through atrocious legal punishments imposed on utterly trivial grounds; and thus, in all aspects of Afghan society they witnessed what we might now call terrorism but to them it was, and remains, a way of life. This is a country where, had no arms been recovered from the retreating Russians 20 years ago, nor any been imported since, every man would still be carrying a gun, for here there are a thousand armourers who can make a reasonably accurate weapon in a workroom where most westerners called Purdy would fail to open a can of beans, and, for the price of a light lunch in The Ivy, turn three generations of a family into a fighting force. This is a country where it is expected of a man to carry a gun without being in any formal sense a soldier, and where a soldier is not a man with a steel helmet, packs on his back and boots on his feet, but a barefoot man in the daily dress of barefoot men, who, in defeat, can fade into the ground in a moment.

Not for these men are there the entertainments of Covent Garden and the Royal Academy, nor the perfumes of Arabia. Water must be fetched and carried and they have so little in the way of creature comforts that westerners, dreaming of the soft toilet paper and pink gins to which they will so easily return, wonder how they bear the hardships. And some western visitors to this neck of the woods, knowing how even the air is thin, are appalled at the random damage that, with Blair's blessing, uncomprehending Americans, well-fed in the absolute security of battleships and bases many miles away, are inflicting on these wretched people in the names of justice and self-righteousness.

If the Afghan has a consolation for his poverty it lies in his religion and, if he is reconciled to the early deaths of his children, wife, siblings, friends and himself; it is because he is convinced of Paradise – the Four Last Things of Christianity are prominent in the Koran and the righteous are rewarded with eternal peace and joy (dare one suggest that Mohammed was in some sense aware of the Revelation and Gospel of St John in his vision of the Word and the Throne, the uncreated things?). The thought of Paradise is considerable comfort to those who have a profound belief in it and is an encouragement to the fatalism that sustains so many Muslims in adversity and death. Why should Afghans fear to be the instruments of death when they have been, and still are, taught that God has the power to overlook every evil deed if he so chooses? And if indeed, as some commentators have asserted, the Taliban preaches a corrupt form of the teachings of the 18th century puritanical reformer Mohmmed bin Abdul Wahab, it is worth remembering that he promised immediate entry into Paradise for every soldier who fell in battle and that his warriors are said to have carried his personal note to Heaven's gatekeeper, commanding immediate entry without question or delay. We talk of fundamentalism as a phenomenon of today, but Afghans seem always to have held to their religion with a fierce and intolerant fanaticism born of having in this world nothing but their expectations of the next, a frame of mind now almost unintelligible in the West though common enough in medieval Christianity.

In the Taliban of today we must recognise the Afghan warlord and peasant of the past. Will any replacement government be better? When Blair speaks of democratic elections in the aftermath of his war, does he really believe that such a device could work with a nation riven by tribal rivalries, to whom assassination is a technique of debate? Every Afghan leader in our history has been a bird of prey. Perhaps Blair, so urgently peripatetic in recent weeks, is beginning to realise that Muslims far less extreme than the Taliban use language rather differently from the westerner, that one can treat him as an honoured guest and send him on his way having told him what he wants to hear, but not what he should know – beyond the Bosphorus politeness veils the truth and Blair should realise this before his coalition crumbles and collapses. Perhaps Blair would be better employed if, like Prince Charles, he hob-nobbed with Osama bin Laden's brothers and learned something of just what it is that has driven this member of a wealthy family at the elbow of the Saudi dynasty to reject it for a life that can scarcely be as comfortable even as that of St Simeon Stylites, austere, ascetic, abstinent and celibate. The pity of it is, perhaps, that though happy to hob-nob with the Hinduja brothers and take their money for the Dome, Blair has made no attempt to understand exactly what it is that, to put it vulgarly, makes this Bin Laden tick. Now, having by proxy (shoulder to shoulder) dropped his bombs and fired his rockets, it is too late for Blair to talk, Osama bin Laden and the Taliban must be doubly intransigent, and the great wider world of Islam, reaching from the west coast of north Africa as far as the Pacific Ocean, is inexorably turning against the Bush-Blair axis.

What a pity it is that the Queen, at the first meeting with her Prime Minister after 11 September, did not say: 'Oh, dear Mr Blair, have a word with Charlie before doing anything precipitate – he can tell you a thing or two about Islam.' Perhaps she did and he ignored her.

ALCOHOL
28 MAY 2002

In all the recent fuss and bother over drugs, hard and soft, take-it-or-leave-it and addictive, pill-popping and mainlining, two have been, if not forgotten, certainly ignored – alcohol and nicotine. Both are addictive, both have the power to wreck health and ruin lives, yet both are freely available without legal or moral constraint and, as they contribute billions to the Exchequer, are not perceived to have compromised the Government's hitherto moralising stance on other drugs. With the manifest failure of this stance, based on that of previous governments and the American model – we now have around 250,000 heroin addicts and 40 per cent of crime is associated with the addiction – it is perhaps the moment to consider our state exploitation of alcohol and tobacco as a precedent for new policies on the supply of every other mood-altering drug, from cannabis to crack.

Perhaps the state should also take the supply of these under its control, make them readily available, keep them clean and (within their own parameters) safe to use and, through sales, make a profit from them. This must surely be a better system than the current free, but illegal market, constantly and wastefully in conflict with government agencies intent on suppressing it. Suppression makes vast fortunes for crooks and turns desperate addicts into criminals. Suppression provides the drugs trade with its driving energy and perpetuates the violence, inhumanity, corruption and profit associated with it.

Put drugs on a par with alcohol and tobacco, on sale in every chemist's shop, with taxes flooding into the Exchequer and we emasculate the illegal business for the benefit of the state. This is casuistry, of course, the old doctrine of equivocation, the argument that the end justifies the means, but it has its point, for, as things are managed now, the state wastes billions in a battle that it cannot win, billions that it could make, not lose, billions some of which could be dedicated to propaganda against the trade and to curing those caught up in it.

Were the state to adopt this revolutionary course, would we have more or fewer addicts? What can we learn from the two unrestricted drugs? Tobacco has been under attack for years, lung cancer its bogey, yet for all the health warnings and television campaigns, consumption is on the increase among the very young, adolescents and young women. Alcohol, however, carries no health warnings and seems inviolable – it is too popular and socially widespread, with too many dependants in the House of Commons and too few passionate enemies there; as with tobacco, consumption is increasing among the young. It is distinctly odd that tobacco, which seems not to reduce smokers to the depths of abject human degradation, is vilified, widely forbidden in public and widely prevented from advertising, but alcohol is not – yet in this country excessive alcohol consumption is responsible for an estimated 50,000 hapless alcoholics.

I have known five of them. No rise in price ever had the slightest deterrent effect on them, no friendly disapproval, no residue of their innate sense of good manners. Four, livers and kidneys protesting at the toxins, died in wretched circumstances – one set fire to himself, another was found dead in the street, mistaken for a tramp, the third had a cerebral haemorrhage on the lavatory, fell forward and wedged the door fast shut, and the fourth died in his favourite armchair with a glass of whiskey in his hand, discovered long after rigor mortis had relaxed. The fifth, only slightly chastened by a professional cure, is now neglecting his daily duty to Alcoholics Anonymous. All in their day were respected, even eminent in their professions, one miserably queer, the others enthusiastically heterosexual.

These friends I saw unwashed, unshaven, stinking; in extremis I saw them trembling, tearful, snivelling with self-pity and incapable of controlling bowels and bladder; all lost their jobs, all borrowed money, all lied, dissembled and denied that they were drinking. They didn't care about dirty and unkempt appearance, didn't care about responsibility to work and family, didn't care about the obvious distress of old friends to whom they seemed to have embarked on man's slowest form of suicide. Their sole and utterly selfish objective was always the next drink.

I do not know what drove these friends into addiction. I am inclined to say that nothing did, no private tragedy, no devastating disappointment; it was simply their inclination and all had, in the beginning, ample means to gratify it. No one could ever stop them once the drinking had begun, no one could counsel moderation, prevent them from ordering another bottle in a restaurant or, at home, opening a second and a third. For none of them was drinking a companionable pursuit – the very opposite indeed, for all became assertive and aggressive in their cups and no companion not equally addicted could keep pace with their consumption.

Alcohol changed their characters. They became detached and distant, except for their occasional need to borrow money, and then they were endowed with Munchausen powers of invention; they fell into morose moods from which nothing could rouse them and constructed artificial barriers to exclude their friends. Dried out in clinics, it was evident in all these cases that some cerebral damage had been done, quick wits replaced by dull, conversation and discussion unsustainable; the saddest thing of all was that their humour was destroyed and they no longer laughed. None could hold a job at anything like the level reached in midcareer; some could hold no job at all.

I recognise that all this is anecdotal and that five out of 50,000 is not a sample large enough from which to draw conclusions, but I find it difficult to believe that the remaining 49,995 are as dapper as wagtails, as merry as cherubs, as quick-witted as Wittgenstein and gainfully employed as chairmen of profitable companies. I am intrigued by two questions. At what point does habit or custom become addiction? And what is the mechanism that in some of us successfully prevents our passing it and losing control, but in others is as useless as a set of points maintained by Railtrack?

The fundamental issue in the business of addiction is that we seem not to understand quite what addiction is. We recognise it when we see it and attack the instrument, but show no interest in the need. Is it related to nature or nurture? Do we become addicted because an addictive substance is readily available, or do we, through curiosity or mischief, seek it out? Is addiction the consequence of copy-cat and peer pressure, or have we, with so much else we do not understand about ourselves, inherited from our primeval ancestors a need to be dependent? If primeval need is the answer, then everything we have so far done to destroy the drugs market has been a wasted effort and we must think again.